ARISE

SIR MICHAEL
PARKINSON

D1144000

ARISE

SIR MICHAEL PARKINSON

THE BIOGRAPHY

CHARLIE BURDEN

JOHN BLAKE

Published by John Blake Publishing Ltd,
3 Bramber Court, 2 Bramber Road,
London W14 9PB, England

www.blake.co.uk

First published in paperback in 2008

ISBN 978 1 84454 634 3

British Library Cataloguing-in-Publication Data:

A catalogue record for this book is available from the British Library.

Design by www.envydesign.co.uk

Printed and bound in Great Britain by Creative Print & Design, Blaina, Wales

1 3 5 7 9 10 8 6 4 2

Papers used by John Blake Publishing are natural, recyclable products made
from wood grown in sustainable forests. The manufacturing processes conform
to the environmental regulations of the country of origin.

Every attempt has been made to contact the relevant copyright-holders,
but some were unobtainable. We would be grateful if the appropriate people
could contact us.

CONTENTS

Introduction   vii

1   A Sporting Childhood   1
2   Roving Reporter   21
3   Meeting Mary   31
4   Time For TV   41
5   *Parkinson*   47
6   Game For A Laugh   67
7   Radio Times   85
8   Gongs Galore!   111
9   On the Move   139
10 A Sporting Future   187
11 Golden Guests   215

Appendices
Television Filmography   245
Awards   246

INTRODUCTION

Maidenhead, Berkshire, has something of a regal air. It forms half of the Royal Borough of Windsor and Maidenhead and is within easy driving distance of the impressive Windsor Castle, the quaint town of Eton and some of the county's most scenic villages and woodland areas. It's a smart place, make no mistake about it. In his famous book *Three Men In A Boat*, Jerome K. Jerome described Maidenhead as 'too snobby to be pleasant'. Just southwest on the banks of the River Thames is the parish of Bray. An idyllic spot, Bray won 'Best Small Village' in the 2005 *Britain in Bloom* awards. It has some fine restaurants, including Heston Blumenthal's The Fat Duck, which was voted the best restaurant in the world in the 2005 poll by *Restaurant* magazine. Another local hostelry, The Waterside Inn, is run by Michel Roux. There are television studios nearby, which gives some hint as to the village's most famous resident. Indeed, his mere presence proves that the damning criticism of the Maidenhead area cannot apply to Bray for there are few more down-to-earth people on the planet than Michael Parkinson.

National treasure, chat-show king and man of the people, Sir Michael Parkinson is arguably Britain's best-loved broadcasting personality. From his radio shows, covering everything from sport to jazz, to his four decades in television anchoring shows, including *TV-am*, *Give Us a Clue* and *Parkinson*, he is nothing short of a legend. As he retired from his extraordinary showbiz career, it was only fitting that he should receive the ultimate accolade: a knighthood from HM the Queen. This was an entirely suitable crowning moment to a legendary career. Despite being honoured by the Monarch of the Land and living in a distinctively regal Berkshire village, however, Michael remains true to his working-class roots and is an effortlessly, genuinely grounded man. He enjoys the riches and fame that have come from his television career. Both allow him access to all sorts of arenas and treats that a man of his background would usually be denied. Yet no one could ever accuse him of turning his back on his roots. This book traces the life of the miner's son from his childhood in Barnsley, where he underwent trials for Yorkshire County Cricket Club; it also follows his entry into newspaper journalism and then national service, during which time he served in Suez in 1956.

After quickly starring as a newspaper writer, Parkinson's relaxed and humorous approach soon won the hearts of an adoring nation when he decided to turn his hand to broadcasting. His work in television, though, was only one arm of a career in media. Before long he was presenting shows that included Radio 4's renowned *Desert Island Discs* and he also appeared on Radio 2 and LBC. The Yorkshireman's robust charm belied a nimble way with questioning that produced some of radio's most engaging moments.

He has provided many of television's most memorable episodes, primarily via his legendary chat show, *Parkinson*. Among the most noteworthy occasions on the programme were interviews with Muhammad Ali, John Lennon, Princess Anne, David Beckham and, of course, Emu. Others he has chatted with include Bing Crosby, Bob Hope, Dame Edna Everage, Peter Ustinov, Shirley MacLaine, Robert Redford, Tina Turner, Tom Hanks, Michael Caine, Dustin Hoffman, Jack Nicholson and Orson Welles. Ingrid Bergman, Bette Davis, Billy Connolly, David Bowie, Tom Cruise, Luciano Pavarotti, Madonna, Elton John, Shane Warne, Rod Stewart, Justin Timberlake, Ray Winstone, Kate Winslet, Richard Attenborough and Olivia Newton-John are other celebrities who have sat on those famous leather seats. The list goes on and on and on.

So who were the most memorable interviewees? When he was the subject of an interview, the presenter himself says his best guests were James Cagney, Fred Astaire, Nelson Mandela, Peter Sellers, Muhammad Ali, George Michael, David Beckham and George Best. Many of these characters, and Parkinson's special relationship with them, are described here. Occasionally, he would devote an entire episode of *Parkinson* to one guest. 'I loved the "one-man" shows. I'm very proud of those, people who had made a considerable contribution,' he says of programmes he dedicated to such icons as Sir Paul McCartney.

The crowning accolade that the Queen bestowed on the chat-show champion was one of many awarded throughout his career, including BAFTAs and a CBE. He won the hearts of an adoring nation, who lapped up his shows and delighted at his words in newspapers and books. The pages that follow paint a complete portrait of the remarkable life of an English legend. They inevitably include his love of cricket, where he was the opening partner for Barnsley Cricket Club with fellow presenter Dickie Bird. Later, he had trials for Yorkshire Cricket Club. He also penned critically acclaimed sports columns and a number of books on sport, including football, cricket and golf. As ever, his natural enthusiasm, warmth and grace ensured his writing was always a must-read, influential affair.

Sport, however, was only the beginning focus of his literary talents. During the 1980s, Michael wrote a series of children's books called *The Woofits* – anthropomorphic, dog-like characters, who lived in a fictional Yorkshire mining village called Grimethorpe. The books were later adapted for television, with Michael quite naturally the narrator, his husky Yorkshire tones perfect for the job. The use of anthropomorphic children's literature by a television personality is echoed by Ricky Gervais, star of the TV series *The Office*, who published the successful book *Flaminals* in 2004.

Unlike some modern-day talk-show hosts, Parkinson

never attempted to become the star of his own show. He felt that a good host should, in many ways, echo the style of a good football referee: essential to proceedings, yet unnoticed. However, many of his guests were just as enamoured of their presenter as he was of them. During a 1974 episode of *Parkinson*, Muhammad Ali told him in no uncertain terms just how much respect he had for his host and his craft: 'I'm going to tell you something now. You are intelligent. They told me I had to come and do your show. You see, you're not as dumb as you look. When they told me I was going to do your show, I was honoured. People like you… I like people to make me think. You and your talk and your [facing the audience] you know, he's a brainy man, he's not just an ordinary fellow… You think it's easy, come take his position. You'll find out that I'm a witty person and it's kind of hard to talk to a man like me. I need people of wisdom such as myself to make me think, [to] keep me going.' Michael replied wittily: 'You've put in a takeover bid for the show!'

George Michael, too, is a devoted fan, as Michael outlines here when he recalls how he and the pop star arranged his post-outing interview. 'We sat down at The Ivy, and his first words to me were, "I've always wanted to get on your show… to think I had to show my dick to an LA cop to do it!" I said, "I'm not writing you a script, but if you say that as soon as you walk on, I'll be home and dry and you will be too. That way, you've raised it, and you've made a joke of it."' One can see how he builds his relationship with guests. He built up a major rapport with singer Robbie Williams when he made his first-ever appearance on the show in 1998. Williams, too, made Michael the star. He told the chat-show host that his mother had a crush on him, and then said to the camera: 'Mum! I'm on *Parky*!'

Meanwhile, comic writer and actress Caroline Aherne keeps a photograph of Parkinson on her wall and journalist Brian Viner says his Michael fixation is a long-term affair. 'I cannot tell a lie,' he wrote in the *Independent*. 'Circa 1978, while my schoolfriends yearned to become the next Kenny Dalglish or David Bowie, I was a Michael Parkinson wannabe. Still am, really.' His fellow journalist Brian Reade was scarcely less fulsome in his praise when he wrote: 'Show me a man over 40 who has never envied Michael Parkinson and I'll show you a born liar. He is one of those effortlessly talented men, like Des Lynam, who takes lavish praise from peers and public in his stride, and maintains a street cred in a profession where smarminess and success go hand-in-hand. Here is a man paid a small fortune to do jobs others would kill for, who has played a starring role in a couple of million female fantasies and who now, at 62, is swaggering back like the Sinatra of Chat to show the lesser talents how it's done...'

On and on come the plaudits from those who know Michael: 'He flirts like mad,' says comedian Lenny Henry, 'I think women tend to flirt with him,' was Julie Walters' view, while Billy Connolly told Michael he was the best audience he had ever had. Even the man said to be his rival, Jonathan Ross, remains positive. 'He is the greatest talk-show host this country has ever seen,' said the BBC star. 'And, I maintain, will ever produce.' After the final *Parkinson* show in November 2007, Andrew Billen agreed in his *Times* column: 'He has left us, and Michael Parkinson has not left an heir. People talk lightly of Jonathan Ross – talking lightly being all Ross does – but he is a different proposition. Ross joshes; Parkinson, before the accumulated embarrassment of the job crushed him, asked questions. His departure, 36 years after *Parkinson* debuted late one Saturday night on the BBC, lays bare the crisis that faces the British chat show. We no longer have one.'

The working-class Michael managed to conquer the BBC by making a virtue of his background, not in spite of it. 'Once, I couldn't have got a job there as a gateman, with my accent. Now, they were on their knees, begging you to join if you had a northern accent,' he once said, adding: 'If I came along today as a 26-year-old journalist and said, "Here I am, I'm not a bad interviewer and I'd like to do a talk show," they'd tell me to b***** off!' Despite his fame, he remains an ordinary man and eschews the showbiz party circuit, preferring the charms of a night in with his family. 'I've only been to three premières and six first-night parties in my life. That world doesn't interest me. The question is: where do you want to be? At home with your family or at a showbusiness party? I prefer to be at home.'

Parkinson is also a generous man. When Sarah, Duchess of York, took on a show in America, it was to her friend Michael that she turned for advice on the art of chat. And one can only imagine that every part of the advice he gave her was gold-dust. For Michael has always been one to encourage others. Not for him the ladder-kicking selfishness of some stars who make it, only to decide that they're all right, Jack. Instead, he encourages and nurtures all manner of talent, be it musical or televisual.

The list of Parkinson-backed stars includes Jamie Cullum and Michael Bublé, both of whom owe their first burst of fame on the UK music scene to the presenter's championing of their work. It's a deliberate policy of Michael's, who feels that television has to return to its roots in terms of which musical acts are featured on talk shows. To his deep disappointment, too much of the selection is, he feels, based on whether the artist is a celebrity, or already in the Top 10: 'In the seventies when I first started, I would have on as regular guests Oscar [Peterson], Woody Herman, Buddy Rich... Duke Ellington was there,' he says. 'All were acceptable in those days. No one would raise an eyebrow and say, "Why are you not having the *Top of the Pops* on?" Nowadays if you suggest somebody like that, they say, "Ooh I don't know... Who? What's he done?" It's sad. There's a generation of people running broadcasting, running television particularly, nowadays who have no musical culture beyond that which exists in the Top 10.'

As such, the show has become an unlikely barometer for up-and-coming musical talent. 'For many within the music industry, the influence of the pop charts is being eclipsed by *Parkinson*,' says Ajax Scott, editor-in-chief of industry trade magazine *Music Week*. But a record company boss was more concise: 'It's all about Parky,' he said. 'There is a warmth to Michael, which makes it unsurprising that he has such a knack of discovering musical talent. Music is the food of love, and thanks to Michael, many have played on.' Not that it's just middle-of-the-road jazz that he backs: he was also an early champion of indie rockers Razorlight, for example.

Despite the eccentricity of the television world Parkinson has worked in, he wouldn't have it any other way. 'With typical Yorkshire pig-headedness I have sought a part of my living in an area of television which is a notorious graveyard for performers,' he smiles. He has few regrets in life, but one is a question that he once asked of a comedian: 'I asked Jack Benny once, and you must always beware of comedians – they lay you, they set you traps – and he was talking about silences, how you play a silence and I should have known and I fell right into it and I said, "What is the longest silence you ever held?" And then he took a minute and a half to look round the room like this, with one eyebrow cocked as if to say what a prat sits opposite me, and of course the audience were in tears of laughter. It was wonderful. I just sat there and I dare not break the spell; I dare not sort of jump in… That was the daftest question I ever asked.'

Parkinson has been accused harshly by a handful of TV critics of being a soft touch during his interviews, a ridiculous allegation for two reasons. First, because it ignores the fact that he was not interviewing war criminals, rather producing a light-hearted and entertaining talk show. Second, because he has always managed to ask difficult questions. 'If it's something incredibly private that has no bearing on their career, no resonance other than one person shagging another person, then I'm not that bothered,' he explains. 'If, on the other hand, they've done something that has had an effect on their popularity or their career, then that's fair game. Woody Allen said he didn't want to talk about the relationship he was having with his adopted stepdaughter, so I had to point out that it had affected his career in a major way, that Middle America just would not buy him after that, so I was going to have to ask him about it. He agreed to talk about it in that context, though he was still pretty reluctant.'

Some cynics have sneered at his success and their accusation that he is a soft touch is unfair. He was not a detective trying to crack a murder suspect, rather the host of a chat show aiming to tease entertaining anecdotes from celebrities. 'I am not interviewing war criminals or paedophiles,' he explained to one such person. 'I am interviewing people whose only crime is to entertain people. I don't see that as an indictable offence. Why would you want to crucify Tom Cruise because he believes in Scientology? You might as well attack somebody who believes in Christianity and the Virgin Birth. Come on!'

However, he does agree that he is not one to necessarily follow the same line of inquiry that other members of the media, particularly tabloid journalists, might. 'If George Michael goes into a toilet and exposes himself to people, it doesn't bother me in the slightest and I don't think it bothers the public,' he shrugs. 'I wasn't very interested in exploring that side of him – I wanted to get rid of it as soon as possible. The newspapers' dominant, prurient interest in people's sex lives is something that disgusts me, frankly.'

Furthermore, he feels that he has never 'backed off asking a really important question with anybody'. As evidence, he points to the awkward interview conducted with the movie star and director Woody Allen in April 1999. There, he believes, is proof that he can balance asking the tough question with agent's demands and with the audience's need to be entertained while making a cracking piece of entertainment. 'I asked him about his marriage to [his adopted stepdaughter] Soon-Yi,' he recalls. 'I was told, on pain of death, not to ask him about that – his agent said he'd walk off. But you couldn't fail to ask him, not about what he did in bed with her, but about the effect it had on his career.

'I asked him about it, and Allen sat there and answered the question and we talked about it, and it was fine. No, it wasn't fine, it was awkward; I'll never get a Christmas card from him. And remember, I've got to ask questions in the middle of an interview, whenever they fit logically into the conversation, and if the interviewee goes, I'm talking to an empty chair for 20 minutes.' It's a tough balancing act, and one he has managed to pull off with seeming ease. As we shall see, Parkinson has asked extremely tough questions of guests as formidable as then Prime Minister Tony Blair and champion boxer Muhammad Ali. Never let it be said that he shirks in his responsibilities as a presenter.

Speaking of his chat bouts with Ali, Michael is a self-effacing man who is never one to brag about his success. Even when detailing his most triumphant career moments, he is keen to emphasise the role he believes fate has played in his story. 'I was lucky to have people like Muhammad Ali on my show five times – he was then the most famous man in the world,' he once said. 'There's been no one like him. And people could see the great Hollywood legends like Fred Astaire. They'd never seen these people in conversation before. When Astaire came down those stairs, it was electric.'

But he is not merely lucky, of course. It's his extraordinary talent, dedication and humanity that has reaped him such extraordinary success during a remarkable career. 'He is just a delight to work with in so many different ways,' a friend and former colleague recounted. 'In terms of professionalism, he is unstuffy and never star-like. He is always assiduous in preparation and is simply never casual in his approach to anything to do with work, and that is the same for his chat show too. To his great credit he has never become intoxicated with his own television myth, even though he is, quite simply, a legend.'

Naturally modest, Parkinson would balk at such praise. However, he would agree that he came of age during an era when the world of journalism was drastically different to the one he retired from. 'I grew up in an era of entrepreneurial men, like the Bernsteins and the Grades,' he says. 'As journalists, we had a basic training in communication but we had to learn the new medium of television without any focus groups, without any instruction books or graphs, only the goodwill of the people who employed us. They gave us the money, sat back and said: "Let's see what happens." They didn't interfere. Now everyone knows everything; that's the way they have to do it. It's a much tougher commercial business. But I tell you, it's not as much fun. Whether or not it's better, I don't care. The kids nowadays won't have the fun I had.'

A household name and indeed an institution, he is also known affectionately as 'Parky'. But it's not a nickname that he is overly fond of and he's not entirely sure where it came from: 'It's an interesting question. I've often thought, when exactly did this bloody "Parky" start? It started at school, and I hated it. I also objected to being called "Parkinson" – as if I was inferior. But "Parky" felt equally derogatory. In Australia, it's worse – I'm "Parko". When I arrived there to work in the 1970s, I came out of the 747 and the immigration officer said, "G'day, Parko!" I said, "Christ Almighty, I thought I was getting away from this!"'

During an interview, Sir Bob Geldof revealed his frustration with being known as 'Saint Bob': 'It got bad when it first started because I didn't know what to do with it at all. I'd always been called several things, Michael, you know?' he said. 'Generally this thing would happen, you'd be walking along a street and older ladies would come along and touch the hem of my garment and they'd start crying. And that was very disconcerting, and they'd put upon you things that you didn't really represent or things that you couldn't possibly live up to and that's, you know, confining and a bit scary. And I wrote a book and that did well, and I hoped to deflate the whole cult of personality that had built up, but it really didn't, but over the years they've got used to me.'

Michael admits his wife Mary occasionally calls him 'Parky' – 'Sometimes she says, "You're a miserable bugger, Parky."' She also claims that on occasion he will put on his best suit, splash himself with aftershave and stand in front of the mirror and say, 'Oh Parky, what a sensation!' 'Okay, I'd say, "Oh, by gum, you're a handsome b*****, Parky!", I still do. But it's only to tease her. To say, "You're a bloody lucky woman, Mary."'

When Michael Parkinson chose to retire, this was considered by many to be the end of an era, not just for the presenter himself, but also for the chat-show genre. He himself admits, 'That's true. My kind of chat show, the kind based on conversation, is finished. Today all the shows like Jay Leno are built around the host and are more about comedy than conversation.' He loved the entirety of his career on *Parkinson*, but looking back over that time, a number of points were clarified for him. For instance, he felt that the guests in the early days had a quality often lacked by today's interviewees. 'To talk to people who'd flown missions over Germany, as well as played Hamlet was to deal with a different creature,' he recalled. 'There was a hinterland, a background, a testimony to having lived a life other than that bounded by the proscenium arch – that's what made the 1970s so rich for me. Today, it's different. Not worse, just different. There are the big stars, but in the main they don't have the texture. They didn't go through a war – and thank God for that!'

Again, he spoke humbly of his success, despite the fact that much of it came about as a result of hard work, rather than inherent ability or good fortune. 'I'm just a lucky guy,' he smiled, as he looked back over his television years. 'How many people have sat next to Pavarotti and heard him sing to them? I sat next to McCartney and he played "Yesterday". How many people have sat next to Henry Mancini and Domingo, and they sang and played "Moon River" together? How many people were there and indeed thought of the idea of putting [Yehudi] Menuhin and [Stéphane] Grappelli together? And how many people had the chance to meet Duke Ellington? And I should be sad about all that? I'm delighted.'

Throughout his career on television, Michael's wife Mary has always been at his side. The two married in 1958 and to this day their union remains heart-warmingly romantic. They have three children – Andrew, Nick and Mike – and eight grandchildren: Laura, James, Emma, Georgina, Ben, Felix, Sofia and Honey. A jovial family man, Michael is extremely proud of all his children and grandchildren.

At night, he must surely sleep easily as a result of his amazing, incredible life. However, he admits that his rest is sometimes disturbed by a vivid nightmare. 'It is a terrible dream,' he says. 'I go into this studio, walk down the stairs and sit opposite a faceless person. I don't know who they are or what to ask them, it's dreadful. And then I hear these awful mumbles come up from the audience. I am literally petrified. And then it ends.'

Of course that dream is as far away from the reality of his experience as it's possible to be. Throughout his career Michael Parkinson has always been the consummate professional. Here is his story.

1

A SPORTING CHILDHOOD

On 28 March 1935, in a modest house in Yorkshire, a national treasure was born. He weighed 7½lb and was delivered by the family doctor at their home in Cudworth, South Yorkshire. Previously the same doctor had brought the boy's mother, Freda, into the world. He was 'an old man who smelled of St Bruno tobacco,' the hero of our story was to remember later on. It's an early indicator of the pivotal place Michael Parkinson holds in English culture that when we turn to describing his birthplace, the most celebrated fact about the area is that he was born there. His star billing is quite appropriate and richly deserved. Cudworth is a village on the outskirts of Barnsley. Other famous people to have lived there include footballer David Hirst, cricketer Darren Gough and athlete Dorothy Hyman (the Dorothy Hyman Athletics Stadium is also in the village). Michael no doubt heartily approves of the sporting heritage of his hometown.

His childhood was largely one of sport, sport and more sport. Writing of his father, Jack, later in life, he recalled: 'My father was a remarkable man with a marvellous facility to adorn an anecdote.' Jack Parkinson was also a keen sports fan. For him, cricket was an enormous concern, almost a religion. 'My father devoted his life to ensuring I grew up playing and loving the game,' says Michael. 'I am glad he did. It is the most English of games, complex and mysterious as Stonehenge; an acquired taste like mushy peas. I was never told fairytales as a child. Instead, I heard of [cricketers] Larwood's action and Hobbs' perfection.'

Given his bedtime stories, it's not in the least surprising that he soon mastered the rules and techniques of this most English of games. 'I could play forward and back before I could read and I knew how to bowl an off-break before I could do joined-up writing,' he recalls. Indeed, he was almost given the somewhat embarrassing moniker of 'Melbourne', as the Middlesex County Cricket Club had just won a Test Match in that Australian city when he was born. His paternal grandmother lobbied hard for him to be given the name but his mother, who he describes as 'a Southerner of great common sense', refused. As for his 'cricket mad' father, he was hoping to name his son after a series of cricketers, including Herbert Sutcliffe, Percy Holmes and Hedley Verity. Happily, he was called Michael.

He might have escaped a cricketing name, but for him there was no escaping a cricket-dominated childhood, not that he would have wanted to do so. Many of his early memories revolve around the sport. He remembers sitting with his mother as the two of them watched his father bowling at the cricket field: 'He was slim, with thick, wavy hair. He had a reputation as a fast bowler – there were not too many batsmen who fancied facing him.' But he finds it hard to attribute these beautiful memories to a particular year and he cannot recall how old he was when these formative events occurred. 'All I know is that when I first saw him play, I was no taller than a Harrow [cricket] bat and weighed less than the big brown teapot they brewed the tea in' – a typical 'Parky' turn of phrase there: English, rich with imagery and quirkily humorous.

Another early adventure came when he found himself lost at Butlins in Filey, North Yorkshire, in 1938, which is his earliest childhood memory. It must have been a terrifying experience for the youngster. He can still see himself sitting on a desk next to a woman who was announcing into a public-address system: 'Would the parents of Michael Parkinson please come before he eats all our ice-cream.' All was well in the end, though, as he explains: 'I remember sitting on a counter next to an ice-cream machine, crying, and then my mother coming through the door to collect me.'

His mother too had long been touched by his father's love of cricket. Michael says that when she married his father, she did not realise that 'she was taking on the Yorkshire County Cricket Club as well.' This would have been made plain, though, on their honeymoon, which his father convinced his new wife should take place in the capital. Not that they experienced much of London's glamour as they spent three days watching Barnsley play Middlesex at Lord's. Michael himself was to later honeymoon in London, but he would spare his wife a trip to the home of English cricket.

Not that cricket was the only sport to capture the youngster's imagination. Indeed, when asked what they remember of him as a child, Cudworthians also recall his passion for football. Where many of his neighbours had balls made of rags, Michael was lucky enough to have a real one, they say. At 5 years old, his dad took him to his first football match. At half-time, father asked son whether he was enjoying the experience. 'It's all right, but I think we'll go home now,' he replied. He would grow to become far more aware – and fond – of the charms of 'the beautiful game'.

As for his home life, to listen to his account of the early years living on Moorlands Terrace, it sounds full of charm. 'I had a blissfully happy childhood,' he recalls. With a typically nostalgic, no-nonsense tone, he adds: 'Nobody interfered with me, nobody tried to hurt me – I was smothered in love, attention, care… But I was also allowed to be a child, as children are not now.' Keen to emphasise the security and happiness of his formative years, he reiterated: 'I had a very, very happy childhood – I only remember with a smile my childhood in Cudworth. I was brought up in a very close mining community and I can always remember being happy, and that's the wonderful thing. I loved the mining community.' That same community was hit hard by the job losses and pit closures that prompted and followed the miners' strike (1984–85). During the 1990s investment was made in an attempt to rejuvenate the economy and morale in the area but this was too late for his father's generation.

'My dad was a miner, and my family were miners, and I was the first generation to get away from that,' he says, before explaining the social changes that he credits with his more liberated life. 'I was freed by the 1945 Education Act, which allowed bright boys to go to grammar school for the first time ever without paying for it, so I broke away. My generation was the one that set up the 1960s. Mine was the generation that created the revolution – if you like, the cultural revolution – and we did that because we were free for the first time. So you weren't able to predict just how far that freedom would go. You knew it was rather good but still the ramparts of the class system in Britain in those days were huge and high and there didn't seem to be any tackle around to get over it, but we did eventually with persistence.'

But before the Swinging Sixties and the changes it wrought came about, World War II began. Thanks to his profession, Michael's father remained at home and he has vivid memories of him during wartime: 'He worked down the pits during the war because it was a reserved occupation. He used to have this Anderson Shelter at the bottom of our garden, and when the sirens went off in Sheffield, we'd rush to sit in this bloody place.' Happily, despite the world being at war, the only casualty Michael ever saw was of the feathered variety: 'He [his father] always used to take the budgie in a cage so we'd know if there was a gas attack. He'd keep flicking it to keep it awake. In the end the poor bugger fell down because it was knackered. It died of lack of sleep, not gas!'

One of his father's hopes was that Michael would one day

play cricket for Yorkshire. The one thing he wished his son would *not* do, however, was to follow him into the mines. To this end, he gave him a memorable experience to try and shock him out of any attraction to mining as a career. Recalls Michael: 'One Sunday morning he said: "I'll show you a pit," and he took me down Grimethorpe Colliery. The ride down in the cage was bad enough, but then he deliberately took me to where there were men working on their bellies in a 3ft 6ins seam and that terrified me. When we came out, he said: "That's what working in the pits is about," and I didn't need any second warning.'

Not that he was in any way dismissive of the miners and the vibrancy their culture brought to the area. He once said, 'I went back to where I was born about a year ago, two years ago, and the landscape of my childhood is gone. I mean, there are no pits any more, the pit gear has been knocked down, the spoil heaps are now grass slopes like little mountains; little grass mountains. The mining community that I grew up in is boarded up. What remains at Grimethorpe Colliery, where my father was, is a pub and you can still hear the brass band that's now being supported by some local industry. But, in that thriving community that I grew up in, and we loved, the laughter is gone.'

Just as his father's profession shaped him, so too did his leisure time activities. Or rather, as he explains, what he did *not* do. 'We were all in the same boat,' says Michael, of his community. 'It was by degrees of poverty that you were judged. The defining factor was whether your father drank or didn't drink. The kids who were unhappiest at school were the ones whose dads went out on a Friday night and got absolutely blotto. My father didn't do that.' In later years, during a lull in his career, Michael admits that for a while he drank more than was ideal. However, he was quickly brought to his senses, as we shall see, and returned to even greater heights.

As for his mother, Freda, perhaps unsurprisingly Michael sees her in quite a different way to his father, although she shared her husband's hope that their son would not go into mining. 'My dad was one of 17 children and he was down the pit when he was 12,' he explains. 'But all the ambition and the volatile side of my nature come from my mother. When I came along she channelled all her drive into me. Her attitude was always, "You've got to better yourself." She said: "You mustn't go down the pits." It wasn't that she was not proud of what my father did, but she just didn't want that for me, and he, God bless him, agreed with her.

'I saw my mother as being different, more glamorous, very creative. I was always well turned out, everything was woollen, Balaclava, gloves, and she knitted her sister's wedding dress in silk. She made up Fair Isle patterns in her head and somebody said to her: "Why don't you send off these patterns?" So she sent them to Patons & Baldwins and the first model was Roger Moore. My mother's still got this picture of Roger Moore wearing one of her McCartney's Fair Isle pullovers. She used to be paid three guineas per pattern and that's how I learned to type because she bought this old typewriter and she'd say, "Knit 2 tog... Knit K1... Purl 1," and I used to tap it all out.' And when he turned his hand to journalism and became an author, Michael was tapping out plenty more than that.

Indeed, it was much later that he truly got a grasp of what his mother was really like as a person. In 2007, when she died, aged 95, he discovered an unfinished and unpublished book that she had written about her life. Reading it proved to be an experience that shocked him to his very core. 'I became aware of the real person,' he says. 'There is a moving account of being totally, utterly broke, bringing me up in this pit village, my father out of work with lock-outs. I felt even more of a heel. Everybody has guilt about their parents, wondering if they could have done better; I never quite understood. I could see why I was happy as a child – because they wanted me to be happy.' It sounds simple but this is not a luxury enjoyed by all children and Michael, always sensible and grounded, is aware how fortunate he was.

As a child, he could see the mining pit from his bedroom window and he remembers the terror when the siren went off, which meant there had been an accident. As his father was involved in such a dangerous profession, rarely were there days when he and his mother did not worry about Jack's safety: 'My mother would just freeze as she was ironing, because there weren't any telephones in those days. She'd just wait, hoping there wouldn't be a knock on the door.' Those fears were by no means irrational because the family had a history of such an accident: 'My father had to dig his own dad out after a fall. My grandfather, Sammy Parkinson, was a character. He used to cheat at dominoes, and when he was playing and bent his head, you could see where the seam had fallen on top of him and nearly scalped him. He had snow-white hair and underneath there were blue scars like the tributaries of the Nile.'

Later, it was not the mining pits that Michael took to as a profession, but journalism. This was an early dream of his, albeit one which caused raised eyebrows in some quarters. 'I wanted to be a journalist ever since the age of 10,' he recalls. 'We were a mining family and they kept saying: "What's a journalist?" It's like saying: "I want to be a Martian."' Those were his schooldays. It is fair to say that he is not a subscriber to the school of thought that school days are the best days of one's life, particularly when it came to his secondary education. 'I just about got through primary school, but grammar school I loathed,' he says. 'I'm talking about 1945, when I was at grammar school and the teachers were these old Victorian masters; it was wartime, and I was taught by sour, brutal old men who'd been brought back from retirement. The head liked beating kids. I got beaten for reading *The Grapes Of Wrath* instead of Sir Walter Scott and arguing that Steinbeck was a better author. I couldn't wait to get out.'

One aspect of the educational system that did meet with Michael's approval, however, was the local girls' school. It seems his eye for the ladies – much remarked on when he often flirted lightly with female guests on his *Parkinson* show – was developed at an early age. 'We were allowed one meeting a year with the girls at Barnsley Girls High School and that was for the road-safety quiz. I was captain of

Barnsley Grammar School road-safety team, which is an indication of how much I wanted to be near girls. I couldn't even drive but nobody knew more about road safety than I did,' he remembers.

Many young men find themselves feeling awkward around women at this stage in their development and Michael was one of them. He was uncomfortable about his appearance, as he told a television interviewer later in life: 'I just thought that I could improve things, and [American film actor and singer] Rob Mitchum was my great, great hero. I used to love the way he could lift the eyebrow. And I used to go to bed at night and I used to put sticking plaster on my eye – I liked that – and also I wanted a dimple like Kirk Douglas, so I'd do that, and I'd stick that over as well. And I used to lie in bed, I used to look like a road accident I'd sort of lie there with this tape all over me. Didn't make any difference.' As it turned out, he would do just fine with his natural appearance. Even in later years, his grey hair and craggy face were to became virtues for him.

By this time, future journalist and author Michael was already making a difference to his classmates – he was being *paid* to write while he was at Barnsley Grammar School. Less able pupils paid him to write their essays for them. Those were his first-ever commissions, though the pupils issuing them could hardly have dreamt that their wordsmith classmate would go on to become one of the most celebrated journalists his country ever produced. Nor did his exam results hint at greatness. He left school in 1951 with just two O-Levels, in Art and, naturally, English Language. Perhaps the latter was at least a hint of what was to come, but a decidedly subtle one. Michael was to be the people's presenter and he would make his mark in the world due to sheer talent and ambition, rather than any letters after his name or as a result of an old boys' network of public schoolboys or Oxbridge graduates.

Away from school entertainment galore was to be had, again much of it sporting. When Michael looks back over the years at his secondary school, he sees 'one long cricket match, interrupted now and then by totally unnecessary matters like learning algebra or conjugating Latin verbs.' Many of those cricket matches were contested on the streets of Barnsley. As he wittily put it in his *Michael Parkinson on Cricket* book, the first floodlit match did not take place in Australia, as is officially true, but rather it was held in the mining village of Cudworth, outside No. 10 Moorland Terrace, where a streetlight was the wicket and where a flickering gas light served as the floodlight.

They were chaotic, but wonderful games, the sort of moments that make childhood so fantastic. In the dark, the batsman was unable to see the bowler as he approached. Meanwhile, with one foot on the pavement and the other on the road, the bowler would run up, meaning the approach would be comically unbalanced: 'This accounted for the appearance in local cricket of certain bowlers whose run to the wicket gave every indication that they were wearing a surgical boot.' By this time Michael was a wonderful batsman and he was once at the wicket for four nights running. There, he amassed a record innings of

1,027 not out. Not even West Indies great Brian Lara has beaten that. However, a friend of Michael's nearly did, scoring 1,010 before being run out when he left the crease to answer a call of nature. They were those sorts of games, those sorts of evenings... No wonder there was such interest and competition in the games, for according to Michael, 'There was not a single person in our street games, not a boy or a girl, who didn't have the ambition to play for Yorkshire. It wasn't so much that you wanted to, as it was expected of you.'

As we have seen, this expectation was particularly pronounced in the Parkinson household, where his father was desperate for Michael to play for his county. It is a trial for any child to go against his father's wishes, so how would he break the news that he was not keen on a cricketing career? He didn't, is the short answer: 'I never told him I didn't want to play cricket for a living; I didn't dare. The truth dawned when I realised a life's ambition and joined the *Manchester Guardian*. Delightedly I crossed the Pennines to tell my parents. Mother was really pleased. Father said, "It's not like playing cricket for Yorkshire."'

However, while he was not playing cricket *for* Yorkshire, he was playing plenty *in* Yorkshire – and other sports too. At Barnsley Grammar School, believes Michael, he learned only two skills: to smoke and to play cricket. Academically, he values his tenure there as 'a complete waste of time'. In those days sport was an important part of the curriculum before the decline in emphasis came along in later years, much to his dismay. As a schoolboy, classroom lessons were mere formalities to get through before the real action took place: the sports lessons. He suspects many of his teachers felt much the same. One such teacher, Webb Swift, taught him and his classmates football and cricket. He was a robust man on the football field, who suffered neither fools, nor fair players gladly. Michael himself admits that he was a 'delicate' player on the pitch and he fears that Swift may have thought him a 'Nancy'. Such a tag could never be applied to Swift, who once put in such a cracking tackle on a pupil that the pair slid off the field and down a bank. Naturally, both Yorkshiremen got up and dusted down, then laughed off the whole thing.

It was during such idyllic childhood days of sporting adventure that Michael first met someone who was to become a lifelong friend and a celebrity in his own right. Born in Yorkshire in 1933, Harold Dennis Bird was to become the most famous cricketing umpire in Britain. Best known by his nickname of 'Dickie' Bird, he has become such a legend that a bronze sculpture is to be placed in Barnsley in recognition of him. It was during his schooldays that Michael first met him. 'I met Dickie when we were young kids, playing in the Barnsley first cricket team,' he says, nostalgically. 'I would have been 14, Dickie 16. He was not the most talented cricketer I'd ever seen but he was determined. Dickie and I used to open the innings and we had one or two long partnerships. My father and his father used to sit together when Dickie and I opened. In those days if you got 50 runs they passed a hat round, and the first person to get 50 got the biggest collection. If Dickie and I were batting together it would be a race to see who got 50 first, and then a race to get to the bar to stop our fathers drinking it all.'

At such a tender age the pair were hardly heavyweight drinkers. Michael describes himself and Dickie – the youngest people in the team – as 'pimples on the bum of Barnsley Cricket Club.' He adds: 'We didn't drink much in those days – one sniff of the barmaid's pinny and we'd be totally riotous! Dickie was a funny, nice kid but he was shy and socially uneasy. He thought somehow that he'd come from a poorer background than most, and probably he had. He was a bag of nerves. He used to chew his fingernails through his batting gloves, and when you consider they were stuffed with half an inch of horsehair that took a certain amount of dedication. Dickie was once, spectacularly and famously, so nervous that he buckled his pads together so that when he stood up he fell flat on his face.'

By that point, it was not unheard of for Michael to take to the cricket pitch wearing a white Balaclava. His 'saintly' mother had knitted it for him in classically caring, maternal fashion. Once she even knitted a cover for his cricket bat: 'I did not believe that my team-mates in the Barnsley dressing-room were ready for such a radical fashion statement and hid it at the bottom of my cricket bag.' Later she would knit him woollen caps to wear on cold days while playing golf.

Not that the strange clothes were a problem for Bird, who loved his friend's down-to-earth nature. 'I went to Raley Secondary Modern, but we played cricket together at Barnsley Cricket Club,' he remembers. 'I thought grammar school boys were little toffee-noses, but I took to Michael because he shared my love for cricket and I soon realised he was very down-to-earth. After school we'd practise in the nets, then sit on the boundary and talk cricket. My idols were Sir Leonard Hutton and Johnny Wardle, and Michael looked up to those great players too. We had other things in common: we were both coal-miners' sons. I'm shy, and deep down Michael is the same. He's had those famous nervous habits of flicking his ear, scratching his nose and putting his hand through his hair all his life. Perhaps it's something about Barnsley boys, because I have nervous mannerisms, too. When I'm umpiring I twitch my arms and tug at my jacket and cap.'

He tells the story of how the pair had trials with Yorkshire Cricket Club well. It's full of boyish awe and enthusiasm, and – ultimately – disappointment. 'Like all Yorkshire kids, we had an ambition to play cricket for Yorkshire,' he says. 'After we left school, we received invitations to try out in the nets at Yorkshire County Cricket Club. It was an honour for any youngster and, as we walked through the gates at Headingley, we could hardly contain our excitement. But I had a terrible time, and so did Michael.

'It was a rain-affected pitch and we were batting against three of the best bowlers the world's ever seen: Freddie Trueman, Bob Appleyard and Johnny Wardle. I never laid bat on ball for 15 minutes and afterwards Arthur Mitchell, the Yorkshire coach, said, "Tell me, what does tha' do for a living?" I said, "I work in the fitting shop at Monk Bretton Colliery." He said, "Tha' hasn't shaped too well here today.

If tha's going to play like that, don't come back. What does tha' mate, Parkinson, do?" I said, "He works on the local newspaper." "I've some advice for him," said Mitchell. "Tell him to stick to journalism."'

Of course Michael did stick with journalism, professionally at least, and all told he equipped himself rather well in that field. Throughout his days at the *Manchester Guardian* and his decades of television stardom, his friendship with Bird has remained strong. 'Michael and I have been friends for nearly 50 years, and have the same relationship we had when we were lads, except we don't see each other as often,' smiles Bird. 'It's difficult with our careers. But we ring each other and have a natter. Cricket is still one of Michael's passions and I see him at matches and dinners. Some evenings we've laughed at cricketing stories until tears streamed down our faces. I've stayed with Michael and his wife Mary, a great Yorkshire lass. They've a magnificent home on the Thames with a boat at the bottom of the garden. I've had marvellous days with Michael and we've sailed up and down the river and talked about cricket – the only thing I can talk about!'

The last word on their friendship goes to Michael, who remains supremely fond of his old friend, even through the eccentricities of his umpiring career. 'There is nothing to dislike about Dickie Bird – he is a superb human being,' he smiles. 'Give Dickie a light meter, low cloud and a light drizzle, and no one, not even the Greeks, could concoct more drama and tragedy.'

In later years, cricketing legend Geoffrey Boycott was a

guest on *Parkinson*. It was a case of one no-nonsense cricket-mad Yorkshireman facing another on the set. Many of Boycott's experiences will have rung a bell with Michael. He told the presenter during the 1978 filming: 'I first played cricket in the backstreets at my home in Fitzwilliam. We used to play down the middle of the street using a manhole for the wicket, and it was there I learnt my best shot – the straight drive – which if it struck right went all the way down the street.' Boycott, too, had a rude awakening when he went for trials at Yorkshire as a schoolboy. Although he had become the best cricketer in his neighbourhood, when he arrived for the trials he discovered that plenty of other fine players were vying for a place at the club. Happily, he succeeded and thus became a star known around the world and thereby got to appear on *Parkinson*, to chew the cud with his fellow Yorkshireman.

Not that life was all cricket and essay-writing for Michael as a teenager. During his school holidays he would decamp to Scarborough and work alongside his uncle, who was a chef. And his succinct verdict on the experience he had with his summer jobs? 'Gruesome!' Many years later he would return to Scarborough with a far happier task in mind and an important question to pop to the lady in his life. Around this time he also developed a love of music, particularly jazz, and it was all down to an eccentric character who lived near the family home: 'A lunatic lived in our street called Freddie Handley and somehow he managed to get these wonderful records from America so I heard Charlie Parker and Dizzy Gillespie before anyone else had a clue who they were.

'Freddie used to hire the bandstand in Barnsley Park. He'd put his wind-up gramophone there and we'd all go along. Freddie used to wear a black beret, with black shades and a "Slim Jim" tie, so we'd all go dressed like that. I even had glasses with slats on them, like Venetian blinds. We were incredibly cool – we all smoked Woodbines and listened to this music; we just stood there in awe. I am a terrible music snob. I saw Bill Haley and His Comets perform their first concert in London. There was Haley, this funny-looking, middle-aged guy singing "Rock Around The Clock", with a bassist who played lying down. I'd never heard tripe like it in my life. I just thought, this'll never last.'

However, as we have seen, Michael was not just a music fan but also a fan of the beautiful game that not only provided him with numerous amusing anecdotes but also pushed him gently towards the media world. Opposite to where he used to stand was a shed and the view of distant hills. No doubt there was the odd day when they proved a more entertaining vista than the goings-on on the pitch. It's little surprise that Michael so loved watching football live: the action on the field satisfied his love of sport, while the banter on the terraces fed his love of sharp wit. Just as he recalls the skill of his favourite players, so too does he remember with a glowing smile the verbal skills of fellow fans. When an opposition player was hit in the groin by a stray football, the crowd would exhort the physio not to wash the testicles, but to *count* them!

Then there was the time in the 1940s when Chesterfield visited Barnsley and won a penalty late in the game. The normal penalty-taker decided to allow his team-mate (and younger brother) to try from the spot. He missed the goal by some margin and a fellow spectator remarked: 'Nepotism, bloody nepotism!' It was only when Michael returned home to his dictionary that he realised quite how funny the remark had been. Often, during his journey home from Oakwell, he would be on the same bus as his football heroes. It was there that he realised he could tap one of them up for an interview.

When Barnsley drew in a big cup tie away to Newcastle United, the local mining bosses realised a certain amount of 'sick' days were going to be taken that day and so they pinned a notice to gates of the pit: 'In order that the management may have knowledge of the number intending to be absent on Wednesday afternoon, will those whose relatives are to be buried on that day please apply by Tuesday for permission to attend.' In the end the pit was closed for the day and thanks to Barnsley's storming 3–0 victory, not many made it in the following day either.

However, by this time Michael had his own sights firmly set on a career that he would be so enthusiastic about that he would not want to take a cheeky day off, lest he missed yet another amazing moment. Indeed, he was lucky enough to be able to combine work and pleasure. Journalism beckoned.

2

ROVING REPORTER

During his teenage years, while Michael's fellow pupils were paying him to write essays for them, he also took his initial steps towards the career of journalism. At the age of 13, he did his first interview. It was with a man called Norman Bone, who made decorations for Christmas trees. Surrounded by men who worked in the local mining pit, Michael considered a man with a career such as Bone's to be nothing short of exotic and so he approached him for an interview to appear in the school magazine. Bone gave his consent, though he wouldn't have known at the time that he was to be the first interviewee to be quizzed by the man who became the King of Chat, interviewing more than 2,000 stars in front of huge television audiences. Bone told him all about the monetary and creative delights of designing glass baubles. Michael titled the resulting article, 'My Visit To A Glass Factor'. Sadly, it does not seem to have survived to this day.

His burning passion for journalism continues, however, and even in retirement, it's more than likely that he will be tapping out words on his typewriter. The profession is in his blood and he recalls exactly where it came from. As a youngster, after watching a cricket game, he noticed a man riding a green bicycle away from the ground. He was a local journalist, rushing back to the office with the day's results. 'I thought that would be a rather good thing to do,' he recalls. This was a pivotal moment in the young man's life. He enjoyed becoming a journalist himself, not least the local scene. 'It taught me many important lessons,' he says. 'Anyone who's had to go into a pub and face a hostile crowd, and try to get information they didn't want to give you, or knock on doors of local people after one of their relatives has died, you very quickly learn a lot about people. And about yourself.'

After leaving school, he was straight on the road to journalism. Quite literally, as it turns out. He describes himself between the ages of 16 and 19 as 'acned, Brilliantined, tireless in limb and imagination'. By this time he was, he says, 'Indentured – which was a form of slavery – as a reporter on the *South Yorkshire Post*. When I was 16, I got 30 bob a week [£1.50 in today's money], 15 bob of which I had to give back to the paper for the honour of employing me.' Michael worked hard to overcome his shyness, though he had a reputation for nervously flicking his hair and touching his ear during interviews in the early years. He purchased a drop-handled, three-speed Raleigh, adding to the mix a pair of metal bike clips and trench coat in homage to his idol, Humphrey Bogart. Each day he would cycle around the distance of a running marathon, visiting pit villages and quizzing anyone he could get his hands on: 'There was a nest of pit villages which I used to cycle round; it was 25 miles I used to cycle, so I've got beautiful legs. I cycled 25 miles a day, every single day.'

Having spent the day interviewing local people, Michael would take his 'beautiful legs' home and type up the proceeds on his battle-scarred, portable Corona. This was in the days before tape-recorded interviews, so he would have to transcribe from his notebook onto the page. There, he would chronicle the various goings-on of such neighbourhoods: births and deaths, court cases, church functions, events arranged by the Mothers' Union and so on. He also turned his hand to reviewing theatre and attended local productions to do write-ups. One time, his pen proved a little too sharp for a certain actor's ego: 'I fancied myself as a drama critic and I wrote a scathing report about a production of *Midsummer Night's Dream*, I think it was, and the local, the man I'd singled out for particular criticism, was a local antique dealer who turned up with an ancient cutlass outside the office at the newspapers wanting to do me serious damage. I left by the back door. Shortly after, I left Doncaster, which is where this occurred.' It is not without irony that Parkinson, who was later harshly accused of being a soft touch in television interviews, should have caused such offence so early in his career.

On occasion, he would read some of his writings out to his parents, eager like so many youngsters are for their approval. His mother, who enjoyed reading, would give him admiring looks if he read out an especially fine turn of phrase. As for his father, well, he enjoyed hearing about people's downfall in the courts best of all and would respond to such reports with knowing wisecracks. 'It was a strange job,' Michael recalls of the period. 'I mean, well what it was, it was glamorous. So what it proved to me after four years of doing this was that I liked it, 'cause it was routine and boring. And I still loved it; I still wanted to be a journalist... So I knew that I'd made the right choice. Maybe for all the wrong reasons in a sense, but I knew I was all right. So from that point on I was very single-mindedly going to be that journalist.'

Around this time he became drawn towards the world of showbusiness. The glamour and creative buzz must have seemed almost impossibly attractive to the boy from Barnsley. 'I used to go to the cinema four times a week. I knew how a New York taxi driver spoke long before I knew how anyone in Manchester talked. In the end, I got to interview the people I'd only ever seen before 30ft high on a screen,' he said recently. The prospect of being paid to exist in that world was an exciting one and he was soon taken by the idea of interviewing entertainment people. His first 'victims', as he termed them himself, were a pair of local entertainers called, to the best of his memory, Denis and Sylvana. 'He was a dark, slim man who wore make-up all the time,' Michael remembers, 'she was blonde, prettily plump, but perpetually sad.' The duo would sing pop songs of the day to audiences at Working Men's Clubs and similar venues. 'I don't know what attracted me to them but I do remember at the time I believed they were the most glamorous, fascinating people I had ever met.'

He watched them perform in front of 'two hundred drunks' at a local Working Men's Club and then, to the surprise of his parents, invited the couple back to his home for a spot of Sunday lunch. Denis's made-up face caused not a little surprise, particularly with Michael's father, who had 'never been confronted by a man wearing mascara and rouge with his mouth full of Yorkshire pudding'. Meanwhile, Sylvana sat, he recalls, in silence and 'mournful concentration'. By the time he met them again he was a shaven-headed soldier when the pair pitched up as entertainers at his camp. They gave him short shrift and seemed even more entrenched in their individual traits – him, make-up, her, melancholy. 'I gave up the world of showbiz that very night,' he jokes.

But he was soon to be firmly working in a showbiz career – on television. Surprisingly, though, the event that led to the most dramatic change in Michael's life to date, which ultimately gave him a huge push towards TV superstardom, happened not in England, but Egypt. Gamal Abdul Nasser came to power there in 1954 and one of the first steps he took as leader was to seize control of the Suez Canal. Previously, it had been a potent symbol of Western dominance in the region. Britain and France were the major shareholders running it and British troops occupied its banks. So, when on 26 July 1956, Nasser opted to nationalise the Suez Canal, shockwaves went across the world. Former head of the Suez

Canal Authority, Ezzat Adel, explains the significance of the Suez nationalisation, which continues to be celebrated on its anniversary each year: 'Of course it is a very important date, not to us as ex-Suez Canal people but to the whole of Egypt's population,' he says. 'It represents a very important idea, which is that the Egyptians were not thought able to run this international waterway and we proved the contrary. Egypt lost 120,000 people digging the Suez Canal by shovels and carrying cases of sand under almost slavery conditions, very little health care, very few wages. Against this very high sacrifice Egypt did not get a fair share of the profits of the Suez Canal.'

Britain, however, was having none of it. When the nation teamed up with France and Israel in 1956 to try and recapture the Suez, Michael was thrown into the fray as the British Army's youngest captain at the time. It was the very last year of conscription. Not that he was exactly in the frontline of the battle, rather, he was cleverly using the opportunity to further his aspirations for a career in journalism. 'I waded ashore at Suez with a Remington over my head,' he said. 'What, a rifle?' he was asked. 'No, a typewriter,' he replied. He recalls being surrounded by 'posh twits' from public schools.

'It was straight out of *Scoop*. I became the youngest captain in the British Army.' He almost cries with laughter as he describes shadowing Robin Day, then a young BBC reporter. 'I was told he was a bit of a bounder and possibly subversive. He told me to p*** off twice.' He says of his time there that his deployment 'shows how daft the British Army were,' adding, 'It took me away from the mining area in Yorkshire, from my womb in a sense, and I was again very lucky. I got a commission, and God knows how, and through a series of mischances I got sent on the Suez operation, where I became the youngest captain in the British Army at the age of sort-of 19?. I had three pips on my shoulder. I mean, such a masquerade you've never seen, oh what a con man! But that put it into a different kind of area.

'For the first time in my life I was mixing with public schoolboys, I was mixing with a different kind of person than the one I'd met before. Hitherto I'd been frightened and quite chippy of those people, I'd imagined them to be different but I realised they *were* different. Some of them weren't quite as bright. And it's a very interesting thing to find out, to discover that you can be put off. In England it's certain you can be by the class structure, it's interesting to come up against it, to find out that it's not really what it seems to be. It's not that big a hurdle if you've got an ounce of talent and an ounce of ambition.'

Positive thoughts, then, about his brush with military conflict; indeed, he insists he gained from his time in the Suez conflict: 'That did me an awful lot of good – it gave me confidence and it moved me into a different area altogether. And because my job in the Army was looking after the press, I was kind of an officer who went round and looked after the media. From that point on, I mean, I actually moved on and upwards into a different realm of journalism till when I left. It was a strange job, actually. I mean, I met many fine wonderful war correspondents. We were covering a war, it was my first taste of a war, and I'd covered about five or six after that as a journalist. I never grew to like them.

'I mean, there's a kind of, there is a journalist and a very fine one too, photographers as well, who actually thrive on war, for whom it actually becomes a kind of a drug and an addiction, and I've worked with them. And they're quite dangerous people to work with in a sense because they don't see the danger that you see. I worked with a photographer called Don McCullin, a very, very fine war photographer, and I did the Six Day War with Don McCullin and he took a very famous picture of the storming of the Mandelbaum Gate in Jerusalem, and if you look at it, it shows a group of soldiers; it's really soldiers, flat out on the floor, doing what men do under fire, which is digging with their hands, they were digging into concrete. It doesn't work, but that's what you do when you're frightened.

'And the enemy, you can see the gunfire coming down from the hill above them. And then you suddenly think, where was McCullin when he took that picture? He was the only man standing up, was the answer, and that's how crazy they are. But that's what they have to do to get the kind of picture to feed our appetite for that thing. But they are different. It's so different for me – I spent all my life being a foreign correspondent in the perpetual funk. I used to sleep in the bath, so I had this fantasy I might be shot through a floorboard. I mean, I was in the Belgian Congo and I remember everyone downstairs getting drunk. It was like the Wild West there, let me tell you. And I was in this big cast-iron bath in the lewd hotel: come in and shoot me, oh God don't shoot me. Oh, it was awful.'

As we shall see, his time in the Suez indirectly gave Michael his first step into the world of television journalism. It was to prove a medium that he would fall in love with, and enjoy working in. But the true love of Michael's life was to be found elsewhere.

3

MEETING MARY

Read any interview with Michael Parkinson, from almost any part of his career, and there is one constant: his wife, Mary. Michael is so gracious in his praise and recognition of her publicly that it is little surprise that they have enjoyed such an amazing marriage. Certainly, the more one studies their partnership, the more one is inspired by their tale. Film director and friend Michael Winner succinctly summed up how the couple met and the success of their marriage: 'When a young schoolteacher in Doncaster, [Mary] was picked up by Michael on a bus. They've been happily married for 46 years. This shows the advantages of using public transport.' That's one way of putting it. However, so heartwarming, moving and inspirational is their story that it deserves to be told in full.

His own summing-up might have been pithy and concise, but Winner's opening gambit was spot-on. 'I first saw her on a double-decker bus,' wrote Parkinson, of the day in 1959 when he met Mary Heneghan. 'I was covering a meeting and she was doing a keep-fit class there. She was a teacher. She was wearing a red duffel coat and the thought idly came to my mind that she had a face I would never tire of looking at. She was sitting upstairs, wearing a red duffel coat. We got off at the same stop. She was tall and slim, with lovely laughing eyes. I was smitten; I was also very shy. I bribed a mate to find out who she was and call her. He made the date and I turned up.' He had found love. As for Mary, why was she attracted to him? He has his theories: 'Maybe it's that I was ambitious and I was driven in a sense, and I wanted to be something, somebody; I wanted to be very good at my job. So we moved. We got married when we were very young, but we moved about 10 times in 8 years and Mary always came with me. We had children at the same time – I mean, it was an extraordinary juggling trick on Mary's behalf, you know.'

The two were embarking on the early stages of their careers and there was a small geographical issue for them to overcome, quite literally, in order for them to meet. 'She was a schoolteacher, I was a reporter on a local evening paper,' Michael said. 'Shortly after we met, I joined the old *Manchester Guardian*. Mary was teaching in Doncaster, the Pennines stood between us.' His new job proved most suitable. The *Manchester Guardian* was founded in 1821 by a group of non-conformist businessmen spearheaded by merchant John Edward Taylor. Announcing the new journal, the mission statement promised, 'it will zealously enforce the principles of civil and religious Liberty ... it will warmly advocate the cause of Reform; it will endeavour to assist in the diffusion of just principles of Political Economy; and to support, without reference to the party from which they emanate, all serviceable measures.' These values chimed well with many of Michael's own views.

However, his job in the north-east meant, as he said, that the Pennines stood between them. Ever resourceful, particularly as his romantic heart was racing, Michael bought an old Triumph for the princely sum of £20 so that he could cross the Pennines to go and see Mary: 'No matter what the weather, [I] crossed into Yorkshire most nights to do my courting. The car had two huge headlamps mounted on a bar. The screws were knackered so the lamps swung loose, up and down and sometimes round and round. Crossing the Pennines at night, I must have looked like a mobile searchlight unit.'

But it was love that he was searching for. As the pair dated – or 'courted', to use the phrase of that era –their love and affection for one another grew. And so came the day when Michael would propose. Having plucked up the courage to pop the question, he did just that at the top of a cliff in Yorkshire's attractive seaside resort of Scarborough, where he had worked alongside his chef uncle as a boy. She said yes, and they married later that year in Doncaster. Michael recalls the day itself as being a strange experience: 'Our wedding day was in a cold church in Doncaster. We'd had a row with Mary's family because I wasn't a Roman Catholic and so her side of the church was unoccupied. The older of her two sisters had instructed the rest of the family not to come because it was what was called a mixed marriage. And just before the wedding, my best man Jim Murray, who was a wonderful Scottish journalist, got pissed. He was arrested by the Doncaster Constabulary going down the Great North Road in a large refuse bin wearing nothing but his watch. He was an old boyfriend of Mary's so he had to get drunk to get through the pain of losing the woman he loved, and I bailed him out.'

The unconventional details of the wedding only add to its charm and romance. Somehow the course of true love rarely runs smoothly. 'Mary's parents were dead so my uncle Jim gave her away because her family had given us the heave-ho. It didn't bother us because we were in love and wanted to get married. But it was a strange day. Mary made her own wedding dress and I borrowed money to buy a suit. We had the reception in a pub and we went on honeymoon in an old Ford Anglia.' (The Triumph had since expired during a snowstorm.).Just as his parents headed to London for their honeymoon so Michael chose the bright lights of the big city for their post-wedding break. It proved a memorable and epochal visit. 'We booked into a hotel in Russell Square,' he says. 'All I remember of the room was that the wardrobe was bigger than the bed, which is how it should be for honeymooners. I knew London well, but Mary was a stranger, and for two days we walked the streets and developed a love for the city that has never diminished.'

Years later, when they returned to the capital for a second honeymoon, they were able to stay in the more luxurious surroundings of The Savoy. 'We walked the same route and laughed at the same things we had seen long ago. Like what? Well, have you ever looked at Nelson from The Strand and speculated just what it is the Admiral holds in his hand? Surely there can be no more serendipitous city in the world than London?' The city was baking, in the grips of a balmy hot summer. Therefore the newly-weds headed towards the West to find more rural surroundings for the continuation of their bliss. They ended up in one of Michael's favourite parts of the world: Salisbury. He describes the city at the time as being 'a cathedral in a meadow'. What perfect surroundings for a honeymooning couple. They had an absolute ball there. For a while they stayed in a pub in Salisbury, then hit the road once more, 'and travelled on through glorious English countryside – the Vale of Taunton and Exmoor – towards the north coast of Devon.'

For the pair, this was unexplored territory. 'I had a vague idea that we might head for Ilfracombe, only because I had seen the resort advertised on one of the beguiling posters British Rail used to commission: "Come to Ilfracombe. The sunny smile in Devon."' However, they ended up in a small village called Woolacombe, where they encountered a man in the hotel car park, someone who was to have more of an impact on their honeymoon than either of them would care for. 'As we drove into the hotel car park we passed a large man with a beer belly and a centre parting,' recalls Michael. 'We were unpacking the car when he approached and said: "Honeymoon couple?" He was looking at the car. I was sure I had wiped away all the tell-tale lipstick graffiti, thrown away the tin cans tied to the front bumper, got rid of the kipper wired to the exhaust pipe.

'"You left a bit of string on the bumper," he explained triumphantly, like some great detective. We must have looked crestfallen. "Don't worry, your secret is safe with me," he said, reassuringly. That night in the bar he kept raising his glass in our direction and winking in a knowing manner. I feared the worst.' Sure enough, later that evening the joker struck. 'We had just nodded off in our four-poster when the door of the bedroom flew open and someone threw a coal scuttle into the room. We both sat bolt upright, at which moment our new-found friend took our picture with a flash camera. The next day he pinned it to the bar. He was a prat and I told him so. Some years later I recounted the tale on television and he wrote to me, saying he dined out on the story. He suggested we meet up to talk about old times. I wrote back and told him that, on the whole, I'd rather be dead.'

Michael and Mary completed their honeymoon far from the balding man's grips. 'Ilfracombe looked just like the poster,' he smiles, remembering their stay there and the train-poster memories that prompted it. 'Looking back, that encounter in the car park is still our most vivid memory of a week in the West Country more than 30 years ago. Funny things, honeymoons, but not half so funny as the people you meet on them.' It had been an eventful, but delightful episode and heralded a marriage that was so happy that it would melt the hearts of the iciest of souls.

Everyone who knows the Parkinsons comments on the

blissful state of their marriage. Here is a story for the romantics to drool over: a couple staying together and growing in love. They lived together and at times worked together, never enjoying being separated for a long period of time. So what does Michael put their blissful and growing love down to? 'She amuses me and makes me laugh. She is very Irish, quixotic, slightly mad, and I like all that. Mary looks even more marvellous as she's grown older, with her wonderful cheekbones and lovely face. She said to me once: "Why did you marry me?" I said: "Because I looked at your face and decided I could look at that face forever."' Both of them cried as he said this.

Not that this delightful tale is in any sense deluded or in denial. Michael admits that both of them have had temptations. He's known to be enthralled by some of his female guests and when Mary appeared on the small screen over the years, she received any number of raunchy fan letters from male viewers. They are also very clear about the fact that there have been rows and at times they have been on the brink of splitting up. 'Of course, we've had loads of rows and we've both thought the other was stupid and been on the point of walking out,' admits Michael. 'Everyone's marriage has been like that at some time. But if you have children I think you have a duty, which is an old-fashioned word, to do everything on heaven and earth to avoid separation and splitting up the family.'

So how would he explain the healthy state of his marriage? 'I don't honestly know how or why it's lasted, I just thank God it has. For all the possibilities that there were to walk away in the past 40 years – and there were possibilities – we didn't.' He has many traditional beliefs and attitudes, and feels that too many people needlessly give up on their marriages. 'People divorce all too easily,' he asserts. 'It's not the paradise people think it will be. I believe you have to make up your mind early on in marriage that no matter what, you will stay together. Part and parcel of two people living together is getting irritated with each other. You have to accept that.'

Later on, during a television interview in Australia, he expanded on the temptations and possibilities. He was asked if part of his interview technique involved flirting. 'Oh, very much so,' he agreed. 'I mean, oh God yes, oh yes. I mean the problem, the problem now, I mean when I first started, I was what, 30-odd, 32 or something like, 33, or 34, and I could flirt with them all, with the best of them. You're on the road, I mean it was fine because it looked okay, but now I'm 68, I mean can you imagine, I look like a dirty old man, should I start flirting away.

'So that's really sort of gone now. I try to be a silver-haired charmer. I'm more thinking now Maurice Chevalier more than anything else. But in those days, I mean, I sat opposite some really beautiful women, I mean, like Ingrid Bergman who I, I mean, I have been in love with her ever since I saw her in *Casablanca* and Shirley MacLaine and people like that, and Raquel Welch, who was possibly the most beautiful woman I've ever seen.' Asked if his famously flirty interview with Raquel caused any tension at home, Michael replied: 'No! No, no, no. Mary knows I'm all talk. Anybody who's been married to a man for 40-odd years knows he's all talk. But the person I used to flirt with most of all was Shirley MacLaine. And she would outrageously flirt. And she once stuck her finger in my belly button, there, and I'd had a button missing, and she said, "We pop 'em off, and the wife sows 'em on." And I think Mary took exception to that, actually!' He joked that he has never since washed his belly button and that it now has lint in it.

So it has been through thick and thin, good times and bad, that Michael has persevered with Mary, and she with him. He is full of gratitude for this and puts it down to honesty and humour on both parts. 'I genuinely thank God we persevered. That we realised, like all other couples, the sublime truth: that your partner isn't perfect. I think only our sense of humour saw us through.' With such a strong marriage, and with so many potential obstacles happily negotiated, Michael feels the pair has now morphed into one entity. There is only one thing that can separate them: death. 'Over the years we have become like one person, indispensable to each other. It's marvellous, but it's bloody frightening because if there is anything that is irreplaceable in my life, it is her. There just wouldn't be enough time left for me to find a similar relationship, even if I had the inclination.'

They say that behind every great man there is a great woman. Michael and Mary's marriage prove this saying true.

4

TIME FOR TV

As we have seen, Michael had much to say that was positive about his experience in the Suez Crisis with the British Army. Another pleasing outcome was that he met Denis Pitts, and it was Pitts who would be connected with his first break in television. Pitts, who died in April 1994, was described by one obituary writer as a 'raconteur, television producer, journalist, novelist and master mariner', and 'always a joy to be with; self-mocking, with a mischievous, but never unkind wit'. Just the sort of person Michael would get along with famously. Pitts presented regional current affairs show *Scene At 6.30*. Michael was invited to join the production team there and once again the pair was working side by side, this time in television.

Among others working on *Scene At 6.30* was a young man by the name of Sid Waddell. He worked behind the scenes, writing some of the scripts for the show. Just as Parkinson has since become a household name, so too has Waddell gone on to become famous, in his case for his charismatic darts' commentaries. Among his hilarious quips are: 'The atmosphere is so tense, if Elvis walked in with a portion of chips, you could hear the vinegar sizzle on them'; 'He's twitching like a Frog in a Blender' and 'When Alexander of Macedonia was 33 he cried salt tears because there were no more worlds to conquer – Bristow is only 27.' Another legend to work on the show was Bill Grundy, who later shot to infamy when The Sex Pistols swore during a television interview that he conducted with them.

During his time on *Scene At 6.30*, Michael first met a band that was to become the biggest in the world and he forged an enduring relationship with one of its members, on- and off-screen. Speaking of Sir Paul McCartney, he said: 'I knew Paul from the very early days of The Beatles, before they made it big, when I used to do a TV programme for Granada in Manchester called *Scene At 6.30*. The Beatles were regulars on that show. It was before they went down to London, made their debut there and changed the world.' Michael, who has always been excited by famous people, must have been thrilled to be in the vicinity of such an exciting up-and-coming band. However, those feelings were reciprocated by one of the band member's relatives, as Michael himself explained. 'My only claim to fame back then was that when they came into the studio to do a recording, miming in those days. Paul's mother once asked me for my autograph,' he smiled. 'She said it was for somebody else but I didn't believe her.'

Perhaps the biggest landmark for *Scene At 6.30*, however, was the day when American President John F. Kennedy was assassinated and the show was the first to break the news in the UK. Terry Dobson recalls: 'As news editor, I took a phone call from the head of the Press Association as the first news report was being received in his newsroom on a live radio link from Dallas. I could hear the US report on the loudspeaker in the background. Because it was a live programme, Granada had arranged a "priority newsflash" arrangement with the PA to ensure we received major news.

'The first brief TV announcement was broadcast almost immediately by *Scene At 6.30* presenter, Mike Scott. We maintained an open line to the PA for the rest of the programme, broadcasting every facet of the developing story. The following day, Barry Heads, the executive producer of the programme, and I received a tele-print message from the PA chief sub-editor congratulating us on an "all-Britain beat" on the Kennedy story.' As we shall see, many years later Michael himself was the first man to break a significant piece of political news.

There were also many humorous episodes during the life of the show. As Ray Fitzwater, former Granada head of current affairs, explains: 'In this Granada there would be openings for all sorts of regional talent that did not previously exist: the Beatles giving their first televised performance, Michael Parkinson being sent off by Plowright to make a four-minute film on rhubarb.' He adds: 'When the Queen visited *Coronation Street*, a well-known actor had been arrested for importuning. David [Plowright, chairman of

Granada] decreed: "The Monarch will meet those members of the cast free from black eyes and who have not been convicted of buggery." When the royal couple arrived, David escorted the Duke of Edinburgh. He spotted that Bet Lynch was wearing a most assertive brassière fashioned out of a Union Jack. The Duke stepped up close, peered down and said, "New shoes."' Another memorable moment involved the Prime Minister of England: 'When Margaret Thatcher visited in 1990 she said to Hilda Ogden, "My name is Hilda, too and I would like to play the part." A voice at her elbow, one David Plowright replied, "And what is more, you will shortly be available."' Cheeky!

Another time, in 1964, Tim Hewat, the editor of *World In Action*, rang Michael with an instruction. When Hewat called, Michael was relaxing on holiday in Turkey: 'He told me, "Go to Cyprus. Slight altercation." I went to Cyprus, met up with the producer and film crew and shot a civil war for 10 days. I get the film wrapped up, get to Nicosia airport [to resume his holiday] and there was a call from Hewat: "Civil war in Zanzibar, get down there immediately." I said, "Tim, I'm in Cyprus." He said, "It's only four inches on the map."

From *Coronation Street* to civil wars, this was a busy time. However, there was more to come. The man with the perfect marriage also played the role of matchmaker for others while he was at Granada. For instance, researcher Michael Apted was introduced by Michael to a former model called Jo Proctor. The pair hit it off and soon married then emigrated to Los Angeles.

The show's legacy lives on. In 2006, television bosses

launched a public appeal for anyone who had recordings of classic television moments for which they had no record. As the *Manchester Evening News* reported: 'A list of TV's 50 Most-Wanted Shows has been compiled to highlight some of the gems which have been lost to posterity. The five most-wanted shows from the Granada region include 1963's *Scene At 6.30* presented by Michael Parkinson.' The appeal was successful and soon rare footage was being broadcast. This included scenes of a fresh-faced Michael being tattooed during a 1962 edition of the show. Also shown were clips of his earliest televised celebrity interviews. One such quiz was with Sir Laurence Olivier. There was also footage of Michael as a BBC war correspondent during the Six Day War conflict in the Middle East in 1967.

He then moved onto another Granada programme called *Cinema* in 1969, a job that he landed as a result of chance encounter with the producer. This was the first show that he had ever fronted alone. It had been launched five years earlier when the original presenter was Bamber Gascoigne and it was a round-up of the week's goings-on in the world of cinema, with clips of current releases. Gascoigne was succeeded by Derek Granger, Mike Scott and then Michael Parkinson. It was a great job for Michael, who had adored cinema since childhood, with his dreams of New York taxis and Hollywood glamour.

The nostalgic television website TV Cream describes *Cinema* as: 'A nuts-and-bolts round-up of the week's big screen business, governed largely by whatever clips Granada had been able to wangle out of the distributors.

Which was usually 30 seconds from a live action Disney natural history yarn or something starring Richard Burton that had been released four years ago. Bamber Gascoigne was the first to fill in the gaps with wry commentaries on celluloid happenstance, before bailing out after three months.' This is a rather unkind summation of a show that was much enjoyed by its viewers, especially during Michael's reign. It was also an influential programme: Barry Norman and then Jonathan Ross have both adapted elements of it for their *Film...* television series.

Following this, Michael began to present a regular afternoon television show for Thames Television. 1971's *Teabreak* was a quirky mix of features and entertainment, later re-launched as *Afternoon Plus* with Mavis Nicholson and Elaine Grand. But not before Michael presented it with his customary grace. On one occasion, he invited his wife, Mary, onto the show. Ultimately, she was to take over from him when he moved to the BBC for his next big break. *Teabreak* was also influential. It was one of a few series that launched the television careers of new presenters such as Mary Berry, Anna Raeburn and Jill Tweedie. The shows were produced by Catherine Freeman and Mary McAnnally.

The career of Michael Parkinson was already in full swing, however. And for him, an even bigger break was just around the corner. Soon, irrevocably and wonderfully, his life was to change.

5

PARKINSON

Michael's Parkinson's presentational skills and easy manner in front of the camera were noticed not just by viewers but also by television folk. Soon, he was invited by the BBC to front his own chat show. It was 1971, it was to be called *Parkinson* and it was to change not just his life, but television history. *Parkinson* became the benchmark by which broadcasters around the world approached chat-show interviews. To appear on the show became the dream of stars across the globe. However, as ever the presenter's brilliance had the common touch and it therefore also became the ambition of many ordinary folk to make an appearance. Many members of the public are happy to admit that they have secretly rehearsed their own debut on *Parkinson*.

So how did this show, which was to prove so successful and influential, come about? 'I wish I could tell you we sat down and planned it, but we didn't,' says Michael. 'I wish

I could say we had a brainwave but that's not the way it happened. In the summer of 1971, there was a gap in the BBC schedules, about eight weeks to cover. In situations like this, TV bosses think talk show! It's cheap, cheerful and expendable.'

But the story is slightly more complicated than that. Richard Drewett, who died in April 2008, was an extraordinarily successful television producer. He'd worked in magazines, and then in 1964, he took a production course at the BBC, just as it was opening its second channel. Soon, he was producing the BBC2 arts magazine, *Late Night Line-Up*, and he gained his first chat-show experience with *If It's Saturday, It Must Be Nimmo*, hosted by legendary British comedy actor Derek Nimmo in 1970. Clive James, who later worked with Drewett, gave a vivid description of how he worked in his obituary of his former colleague that appeared in the *Guardian*. 'It is in the office, not in the studio or on location, that even the most hands-on producer does the work that makes the difference,' he wrote. 'Richard was the executive producer for every programme with my name in the title between 1982, when I left Fleet Street to go into television, and the turn of the millennium, when I left television for a retirement which would be a lot harder for me to make sense of if he had not taught me so much about the fruitful use of time. On top of his charm and good manners, that was the thing that ruled all the other things he could do. He was mad about his family and fast cars, but when he was working he was perfectly sane: far too sane to be interested in power, which he could have had but didn't care about. He cared only about getting good programmes made.'

A trip to the US in 1971 proved to be Drewett's Eureka! moment in regard to the launch of *Parkinson*. While there, he watched *The Dick Cavett Show* and was convinced the same format could work in the UK. *The Dick Cavett Show* was first launched in March 1968 on America's ABC network. Cavett's shows are a mix of chat, music and laughter. He once wittily told the studio audience: 'I have some good news and some bad news for the balcony. I'm not going to tell you the bad news, but here's the good news. It will take several minutes for the flames to reach you.' Such moments are typical of his style. The show has run for over five decades across several networks and has made Cavett a hugely popular figure. Drewett was convinced he could make a similar series work in England but for that, he needed a personality and Michael was his man. He went on to produce the first 132 editions of *Parkinson*.

With characteristic Yorkshireman stubbornness, Michael once wrote that he has sought a livelihood in a television genre 'which is a notorious graveyard for performers,' rather than the springboard to bigger projects. He compares the talk-show host with the late motorcycle daredevil Evel Knievel: 'In other words, it is not necessary to have a slate loose to host a talk show, but it certainly helps.' He might not have had a slate loose, but Michael was already developing the thick skin required to survive in the broadcasting world. At this stage he had already received a less-than-glowing review for his first TV appearance.

He admits that following his début on television he expected to be instantly recognised; he walked, he says, 'with a lusty swagger'. However, the most dramatic thing that happened when he crossed the road is that he was nearly run over by a double-decker bus. Then he walked into a pub and it was there that he finally received the look of recognition he craved. 'There's been a youth on telly just now looked exactly like you,' the barman told him. 'Don't be disappointed,' he continued, 'yon fella on television were bloody terrible!'

During the 1980s he received another rude awakening, this time from a producer called John Bromley. 'We worked together at London Weekend Television where, along with Jimmy Hill, he began a revolution that changed the way we televised football,' Michael recalls. 'I was in charge of a rather po-faced sports magazine programme at the time and fancied a crack at presenting a live programme. Dickie Davies was sick one weekend so John let me stand in on *World of Sport*. To say I was inept was being kind. I was hopeless and ever since have been in awe of Coleman, Lynam, Bough, Rider and all the rest who manage to make an impossible job look easy.' He continues: 'I came out of the studio feeling absolutely wretched. John waited with bottle of champagne in hand. We drunk that and started on another in morose silence when I said to him, "Why champagne? I was bloody terrible." "I always suspected you might be and I am celebrating being proved right," he said.'

Harsh words. And with *Parkinson* he was to face far greater scrutiny. Thankfully, he had a strong production team around him, including John Fisher and Richard

Drewett, who, further down the line was to became known as the 'Godfather of Chat Shows'. The agreed format for *Parkinson* was set fairly quickly and rarely changed as the decades rolled on. During the 1970s the house band was led by Harry Stoneham, who also composed the theme tune in the basement of the BBC Television Centre in London's Shepherd's Bush. The band featured Who guitarist Pete Townshend's father Cliff on saxophone and their theme tune became increasingly familiar.

The set, too, was familiar. Choosing a stylish, yet simple design from the start, Michael admits that as the years went on, he became increasingly 'pernickety to the point of being obsessive,' about the positioning of the chairs on the set's stage: 'I've done so many talk shows where you are sitting down with your knees on your bloody chin and you can't see anything, or the guests have to lean forward to see the host, or there's a desk between them, which is never a good idea. A lot of thought has gone into the kinds of chair we have and the positioning of those chairs.'

He quickly gained a reputation as a host who truly put in the hours to research his guests thoroughly. Unlike some of the later hosts, who seem content to get away with a few jokes and to make the interview about the quizzer rather than the quizzed, Parkinson gave his guests – and viewers – the courtesy of proper research. 'I've learnt over the years how to assimilate research,' he said. 'You can't just laboriously read a book, you've got to be able to cope with reading two or three books in a week for research purposes, never mind a pile of documents.'

From the start of *Parkinson* in 1971 right through to the 2007 finale, this was his policy. Hours spent in research paid dividends. Not only did the guests respect his courtesy, but in turn the viewers were treated to more insightful interviews. This perfectionism led to a high turnover of researchers, however. 'We have a fairly high attrition rate when it comes to researchers,' revealed producer Chris Greenwood. He admits that part of the fascination of *Parkinson* was that it didn't matter how carefully he selected the guests, or how hard he worked on research and preparation, there was no guarantee that any particular show would be a success: 'Sometimes it's a simple matter of a group of people just not liking each other; on other occasions drink and other mind-numbing substances have had a definite effect on the proceedings.'

More often than not, everything clicked and the show proved fantastic viewing. When he was later asked how he mastered the art of interviewing, Michael was somewhat evasive: 'It's in the lap of the gods,' he said. 'It really is. There's no way you can create a chemistry when none exists: there are many times I do a straightforward, professional interview; other times, when there's a real relationship, when the interview becomes conversational, intimate, when you get the impression you're eavesdropping... that's when it works.'

But he was clearer about the starting point for his interviews: 'We all sit and wonder, why is that person famous and not me? And that's the start of the interview, basically. You're finding out on [the viewer's] behalf. There's no conclusion you could come to, no analysis you could make that would prove anything except the feeling I have, that no one I've ever had on my show had it given to them. They all wanted it very badly and they all wanted it from a very early age. And they all worked that bit harder than anybody else to get it.'

The first edition of *Parkinson* in 1971 drew 9.5 million such viewers, leaving the presenter understandably 'delighted'. He added: 'I shall always remember that, because you always remember your first important show, the figure, people who watched it.' Yet surprisingly and tragically, no record of that first series remains. 'The first series of the show was wiped on the orders of a BBC committee set up in those days to decide what should be kept in the archive and what should be rejected,' he recalls, somewhat sourly. 'Now you can tell just how in tune with popular culture that committee was when I tell you it got rid of interviews with John Lennon and Yoko Ono, Peter Ustinov, Benny Goodman, Spike Milligan and Orson Welles from that first series.' This glittering galaxy of stars was, as Michael observed himself, a long way 'from that cluster of pit villages' where he grew up and cut his journalistic teeth.

Looking back at the early years, in his excellent book *The Best Of Parkinson*, published in 1981, he says that the talk show is 'an unnatural act between consenting adults in public. The interview is unnatural because the interviewee is expected to have an intimate chat with the host while surrounded by a million pounds' worth of technology, with a microphone pointing at every orifice, watched by five hundred people in the studio and untold millions at home.' Surprisingly, however, it does often work. With Bronowski, Arlott, Muggeridge, Miller, Welles, Ustinov and some less well-known personalities, they are able to entrance an audience in a web of words and ideas to the point where every single person believed that the conversation is directed at them alone.

Indeed, one of the earliest personalities to cause such a stir was Orson Welles. Michael remembers his joy at booking such an epochal guest: 'We thought, if we can get Orson Welles, the rest will follow – bill it and they will come. And we were right.' Not before some drama and humour, though. He recalls how Welles was just as commanding a presence off as on screen. 'He played a very important part in the development of the *Parkinson* show – indeed, without him it might never have happened. We were given an eight-show series, some replacement, and we tried to get people. And the problem is unless you're actually an established host, the best people, the top people, won't come on. We thought this one person who will actually clear the way for us, if we can get Orson Welles, the rest will follow.'

And he was right. At the time, Welles' reputation was second to none. Michael's producer flew out to Spain, where the director was making *Don Quixote* – the film he never finished – and spoke to Mr Welles and did the deal. 'The deal was this: apart from the money, that he would fly to England, do my interview, providing we knocked the first two rows out of a BA jet so he could lie on the floor and sleep on a mattress.'

For the first time ever, British Airways were persuaded to remove the seats and install a long seatbelt which would reach down to the floor and, more importantly, encompass the large man's 20-odd stone frame. 'And he walked on the aeroplane and he looked at the mattress on the floor and smiled, and went and sat in the seat... And then he came to my room and I'd been working on this interview for, like all my life, and I opened the door and he was dressed entirely in black: black sombrero, black tie, black shirt, black cloak – and he swept into the room, incredibly dramatic. "My name's Orson Welles," he said, "and you would be?" And I said, "Er... Parkinson." "Yes," he said, and he looked around, and he saw this scrap of paper on my desk and he said, "That?" I said, "My questions." "Do you mind if I look?" I said, "No." And he picked them up, and he turned to me and he said, "How many of these shows have you done?" I said, "Two." "I've done many more," he said. "will you take my advice?" I said, "Certainly," and he ripped up the questions and said, "Let's talk," and walked away. And he sat down and he did two hours that night, that were majestic.'

He says of Welles, 'Of all the great stars the most interesting – articulate, witty and fascinating.' In that first interview he recalled coming to blows with Ernest Hemingway during a read-through: 'You have the picture of the Spanish Civil War being projected on a screen, and these two heavy figures swinging away at each other, and missing most of the time... The lights came up, we burst into laughter, and we became great friends,' Welles giggled. Both host and guest were enjoying their chat.

Of Hollywood's tinseltown, Welles was far less enamoured, however: 'I suddenly thought to myself, why do I look so affectionately on that town? It was because it was funny and it was gay, and it was an old-fashioned circus and ah... everything that we're nostalgic about made it funny and gay when it was really happening, but really it was a brutal place. And when I take my own life out of it and see what they did to other people, I see that the story of that town is a dirty one and it's record is bad.'

Michael remains convinced Orson Welles was the turning point in making *Parkinson* the success it went on to be. He enjoyed quizzing him, 'and of course from that point on, the doors opened because agents said, "Well, if Orson Welles will do the show, my guy can do the show." So I owe him a great debt.'

One of the most memorable stars to walk through those doors was Shirley MacLaine. Michael asked her: 'Have you ever been guilty of using the fact that you are an internationally known star to your advantage?' With a cheeky glint in her eye, she replied: 'Yeah, I make your show better!' Such flirtatious banter was far from unheard of between Parky and his female guests. When Bette Midler appeared, he asked her about her Hawaiian roots. 'Can you do the hula-hula?' he asked. 'Of course, I can do the hula-hula. Can you?' she replied. Michael's answer was a straightforward: 'No.' Quirky, flirty exchanges like this were commonplace during the early years of the show.

However, when Raquel Welsh pitched up on *Parkinson*, the discussion was somewhat more sombre. The actress disclosed

56

that of late she had been working hard not to take herself seriously. She said that she felt that more people should try and put their troubles to one side and just enjoy life. Turning to feminism, she said, 'Women's Lib think that being a sex object is a dirty word, and I don't agree with that. They have a number of strategical tactics that they're trying to use on the public to win a certain attention for themselves. What they really want, I think, is fair payment, and something having to do with the evolution of the general mentality that makes women stop competing with women, and men and women relating to one another without playing too many games.'

Looking ahead, she was, she felt, a 'little bit closer to checking out'. Not that this was something that was welcome to her. 'I don't like the idea of checking out because I have a pretty good life and I think it's hard for women to grow older and to think they're competing perhaps with millions of girls with new sets of equipment. But really, I don't know, life has a funny way of compensating for all those things. At least, I hope when I get there that it will.'

Shirley Temple, too, was hopeful when Michael asked her about the future, albeit for different reasons. She had been working with the UN for peace in the Middle East and said, 'I hope things work out. I don't think the world will ever know peace, complete peace in all countries. But I think the building blocks of peace are moving into shape and I think that the world is going to be a better place and a calmer place. I hope for dignity in man, you know, so that people can achieve the dignity and not suffer from hunger and want, and so forth.'

Michael has spoken of his joy at meeting and interviewing comedians during his career. Billy Connolly remains a favourite. He describes him as, 'More of an alchemist than a comedian, a man who takes everyday life and turns it into something funny.' Connolly went on to become something of a popular guest on *Parkinson*. However, there were memorable appearances from other comedians during those early years. One such guest was Les Dawson, who gave an interesting account of what comedians could get away with during the 1970s: 'I think people laugh at the same things now that they laughed at years ago. I think that in this era, you know, of permissiveness, you can be a little more risqué than you used to be years ago, but I won't be dirty and I won't use dirty words.' Asked whether he analysed what was funny, Dawson brushed the question aside. 'How can you analyse what is funny?' he responded. 'If something tragic happens to you, other people will sympathise, but it's your problem. The same with humour, what is funny to you is a personal thing.'

Another comedic guest in the early days was Rowan Atkinson, who revealed how he became a comedian: 'There's no real showbiz heritage in my family at all – it's strange, except my grandfather used to own cinemas and theatres in the north of England,' he said. 'So there was no particular reason why I should have turned out the way I have, except I remember when I was about 11 or 12 standing up and doing some strange things in the school changing-room that used to drag people down and have them laughing at me. Then the adolescent self-consciousness set in and I never dared stand in front of my friends and make them laugh again. I've never done it to this day.'

Michael asked what was the most fruitful ground for him as a comedian and writer. 'It's the very ordinariness of life that I enjoy watching,' Atkinson replied. 'I've never consciously copied anyone. Characterisations you've seen might have been based on people that I might have seen ten years ago, but I can't remember for the life of me who they are, their mannerisms and things. It sounds like an old cliché derived from an old cliché – you know, truth is stranger than fiction – and actually it's just the way the person sitting opposite you on the train behaves.'

Then came comic acting legend John Cleese, who gave yet more insight into the craft. The star of *Fawlty Towers* told Michael: 'In spite of all this wacky madcap humour I do, I actually do it by numbers so I'm really almost over-disciplined. I'm uptight as a performer, much too uptight – visual humour, gestures get across much faster. Gestures are faster than a sentence and oddly enough, when people at home think back to great moments that really made them laugh, they are visual. They are quicker, that's why. With visual humour, what's more, you can hit someone three or four times very quickly.'

Throughout the run on BBC and ITV, *Parkinson* always had its funny moments. The early years set the scene for this. Actress Sarah Miles had the audience in stitches as she described the 'very fuzzy pubic hair' she had on her head as a child and 'the ears that stuck out and flapped in the wind'. On the subject of nude scenes, she had one rule: she would do anything as long as the camera crew also did it. 'As long as they strip off, I'll strip off,' she said. Artist Terry-Thomas also spoke about nudity. He told Michael: 'Full-frontal nudity, 'specially if the subject is a man, just embarrasses me slightly – I can never quite get used to it. I'm terribly inhibited by these things and I feel that, you know, if I didn't wear anything somebody might come up and ask me for an autograph and I'd have nowhere to put my fountain pen.'

Given Orson Welles' damning verdict on Hollywood, Richard Burton's was somewhat more positive. 'Hollywood, it's fantastic suburb,' he smiled. 'It has no centre, no mood. It goes on and on. Nothing but swimming pools and tennis courts, and very rich people and very nice people too, I may say. Or at least to me.' Sarah Miles, too, was positive about tinseltown, 'because everybody was so kind.' Even early on, *Parkinson* was throwing up interesting contrasts.

Michael was also adept at drawing rich imagery and fine words from his interviewees. Jackie Stewart described how in driving, he is 'so close to everything. You know, in a way, it's life and death... I promised that I'd never get back in a racing car and I never will...The chequered flag's gone down, and it's going to stay down.' Michael Caine spoke of his background: 'I think that cockneys are almost a race but what they definitely are is a frame of mind, which means that you recognise each other by the way you take things – you never take things seriously, especially dignity and pomposity – and one of the things about them is that they are very sharp. There is a natural quick wit, which must be a survival thing. If you are a cockney, you are working-class. I mean, you can't be a cockney lord, although there are some now. Usually you speak very quickly because no one listens to you; you move your hands a lot because you try to attract attention. Have you ever noticed that aristocrats stand with their hands behind their backs and speak very slowly because they know that they have got everyone's attention?'

Michael readily admits that some of his shows were compromised by guests a little worse for the wear: 'Elliott Gould and Donald Sutherland are not two of my favourite people because they came on and they thought they were on a rocket ship when they arrived. Mr [Robert] Mitchum was another one. He was fairly out of it, although I enjoyed him. He was funny, despite being negative.'

Michael describes the ideal talk show as being like a very successful dinner party: 'The viewer pulls up a chair and looks over my right shoulder at someone they've always wanted to meet. And the interviewer, as the perfect host at a dinner party, has but one task: to bring out the best in his guests and not treat them like a captive audience for a display of his own wit and opinions.' Having set out thus, he certainly made a success of his plan. Millions of viewers were keen to come along to this televisual 'dinner party'.

Speaking of the birth of *Parkinson*, and the way it turned out, Parkinson said: 'So they gave us an eight-show stint and we fooled them: we just kept on going!' They did indeed. In fact, the show was on our screens for 11 years for its initial run and regularly entertained a huge share of the television audience. One of the most entertaining episodes for viewers, though not for Michael, came in 1976 when Rod Hull and

Emu made an appearance. During an initially standard interview, Hull explained how his Emu puppet came into being: 'I was doing a large show in Australia and someone sent me a large emu's egg,' he explained. 'I put it on the radiator and it grew steadily until one day there was this knocking sound and it hatched, and that's where I got my idea for my Emu from. I have an extraordinary relationship with Emu and he does things which I secretly want to do, but I'm a bit of a coward. All the things I would love to do with people, Emu does for me because who is going to punch an emu? Like going into a supermarket, haven't you ever wanted to go in and knock over all the piles of tins and toilet rolls? Well, I did it with Emu and it was ever so good!'

All seemed to be going swimmingly, though Hull's words about Emu doing naughty things on his behalf should have perhaps served as a warning. Then another warning sign came when Hull said that Emu was very happy in the studio, but that he was not sure why Emu was looking at Michael in such a suspicious way. 'He really is very friendly,' Hull promised, 'he really isn't at all aggressive, once you get to know him!' The bird then lunged for Michael, pecking at his seat and spinning the seat round at great speed. Emu then went for his leg and then his neck. Soon both men and the bird were on the floor scrapping, and Michael lost his shoe in the mêlée. As he attempted to control himself, he was heard to mutter, 'That silly bloody bird!' The fighting then broke out again, with Michael seeming to lose patience with the gag. As hostilities broke up, he said: 'I knew we shouldn't have booked it!' He was genuinely annoyed at the encounter, later describing it as 'a physical assault'. One of the production team admitted: 'It made such a mark on Michael Parkinson that to this day he is reluctant to talk about the mauling.'

Not that he was the only public figure to get a mauling from Emu. At a Royal Variety Performance, Emu snatched a bouquet from the Queen Mother and ripped it to pieces. 'I think your Emu is hungry,' said a startled Queen Mum. Other celebrities to have had a run-in with the feisty bird include GMTV presenter Lorraine Kelly, entertainer Larry Grayson, comic actor Rik Mayall, comedienne Faith Brown and Mancunian TV presenter Terry Christian. Even former Prime Minister and self-styled 'Iron Lady' Margaret Thatcher was not given a reprieve from the puppet's aggressive beak. During a House of Commons party in 1985, Emu lunged at a cake that the Prime Minister was eating. However, the lady who was not for turning was also not for surrendering her cake easily. With all the passion she showed in holding onto the Falkland Islands, she tenaciously held onto her cake and refused to surrender it.

When Emu returned to our screens in 2006, the press all covered the story, leading on the Michael Parkinson angle. DON'T TELL PARKY. BUT THE DREADED EMU'S BACK IN TOWN said the *Daily Mail*. It was a great promotion for the new series of Emu, but this time around there was to be no appearance on the *Parkinson* show. 'The trouble is, Parkinson blankly refuses to have him on,' said Christopher Pilkington, executive producer of the show. 'He has a sense of humour failure about the whole thing and still blames Emu for his bad back. He doesn't want to risk another attack.'

When news broke of the death of Rod Hull in 1999, however, Michael was gracious: 'I am very sad to hear of Rod's death. He was a very charming, intelligent and sensitive man – quite unlike the Emu. The Emu was the dark side of Rod's personality, and very funny, provided it was not on top of you. He was a gentle man and a very endearing companion. He made me laugh an awful lot and we will sorely miss him.' Not that this would ever change his opinion of Emu. He once said, 'The only thing I'll be remembered for is being attacked by that [shower of asterisks] Emu! I hope I never see that damned bird again.'

The Emu/Parkinson face-off has gone down in television history and become a much-cited moment. As a report in the *Guardian* put it: 'The night on *Parkinson* when Emu pulled down the mighty from his seat has been voted number 13 in TV's Greatest Moments. That is 17 places above Charles and Diana's wedding. From the moment Emu started to whirl him round in his chair, it was obvious that Parkinson was not enjoying the ride. If there was a bluebird going, he was failing to find it. None of this had been in his script. Which Emu had, in any case, already eaten.'

Also notable was the appearance of comic actor Peter Sellers on *Parkinson*. 'I remember Mike kept pushing Peter Sellers to come [on the show], but he was nervous,' Chris Greenwood says. 'In the end he would only come on if he could dress as a German, with a helmet and everything. So he did, and Mike interviewed him as a German.' This made for a curious, but entertaining show as Sellers later removed his mask and gave a more conventional interview.

So how did Parkinson continue to pull off such amazing exchanges? Writing in Australia's *Sun Herald*, journalist Felicity Robinson analysed his interviewing technique: 'As the cameras unblinkingly record his every move, he has only a few moments to make his guests feel at home. So he makes eye contact, unbuttons his jacket (one sociologist claims this signals openness) or shifts a little in his seat, and lobs an easy question to the guest.' Parkinson says it's instinctive behaviour, honed by years of practice. 'I think you must learn how to interview but the reason why some people are better than others is about a capacity they might have for settling people,' he says. 'I think it's about body language, it's about convincing people they should be comfortable with you.'

Guests would be feeling comfortable with Michael for many years to come.

6

GAME FOR
A LAUGH

In 1972, Michael became the face of a rather unorthodox campaign. He was interviewed by *Cosmopolitan* magazine about his recent decision to have a vasectomy. The magazine declared that a vasectomy was 'The most beautiful thing a man can do for a woman.' As for Michael, he talked down the suggestions that having a vasectomy can cut back on a man's sex drive. He boasted, indeed, that he was 'randier than ever' since he had his vasectomy. Explaining the decision, he said: 'We had all the children we wanted and it seemed to me that in that situation the alternatives – a major operation for her or the risk of another child we hadn't planned – were too gruesome to be contemplated. Whereas for me it would be just a little snip and no more problems . . . and it's not turned into a prune and I feel fine.

'The only painful aspect of it was the publicity. The news got out because somebody working with the doctor who performed the operation tipped off a magazine. It was intrusive, but on the other hand I think it persuaded a lot of men to think about it. At that stage they often believed it meant having your whatsit chopped off, which only revealed their ignorance.' He went on to explain that he received a lot of mail from the public after news broke of his vasectomy. Some of it was supportive, some of it not. 'One man, a famous old English cricketer who'd never liked me, wrote to me, saying: "Had I known, I'd have done it for you with a pair of bricks." At least he had the courage to sign his contribution. Plenty of others were unsigned.'

Also in 1972, Michael branched out and, in addition to *Parkinson*, he appeared on *The Movie Quiz*. Going out at 6.40pm on BBC1, the show featured Sylvia Sims and Michael Parkinson on rival teams, answering questions about the world of films. Again Michael thrived under the televisual spotlight and viewers lapped up the tea-time fun. Indeed, so good was he in the game-show format that, further down the line, he was to be invited to compete in another such programme, one that was to become even more successful.

Before turning to that he was given a rare honour when he featured on the cover on a solo album by former Beatle Paul McCartney. *Band On The Run* by Paul McCartney & Wings was released in 1973. Alongside other celebrities of the day – including Kenny Lynch, Paul and Linda McCartney, James Coburn, Clement Freud, Christopher Lee, Denny Laine and John Conteh – Michael was shown acting out a jailbreak. McCartney said the concept was 'just a bit of a laugh.' For

Michael, though, it was both a laugh and an honour to be depicted on the cover of one of his hero's albums.

His next foray into the world of the game-show came with *Give Us A Clue*, first launched on ITV in 1979. It had a simple and winning format: a televised version of charades, the popular word-guessing game. There were two teams of celebrities: one was a women's team, the other a team of men. The contestants used mime to demonstrate a name, phrase, book, play, film or TV programme. Sometimes, if their team got really stuck, they would have to mime out a word, syllable by syllable. Contestants were given two minutes to act out their given subject in front of their team. Lionel Blair was the first captain of the men's team, Una Stubbs headed up the women's team.

The original host was Michael Aspel. A high-profile television personality since the 1960s, Aspel has enjoyed a distinguished career presenting favourite family television shows including *Crackerjack*, *Aspel & Company*, *This Is Your Life* and *Antiques Roadshow*. Born in Battersea, London, like Parkinson, he too had done national service before moving into full-time journalism. He was therefore a fine choice and he remained at the show's helm until 1983 when Michael took over. Under Parky's reign, *Give Us A Clue* developed a fine series of running gags and in-jokes. For instance, contestants would often go to great lengths not to use their private parts as part of a mine, with amusing consequences.

Likewise, Michael would occasionally provide a deliberately impossible title for one of the captains to act out. One such stinker, given to Lionel Blair, was *A–Z Of Horse*

Diseases And Health Problems: Signs, Diagnoses And Treatment. 'I think you're going to enjoy this one, Lionel,' tittered Michael, before handing over the impossible. Blair would always take these challenges in good spirit and speaks of 'fond, fond memories' of his time on the show. 'I was captain for 12 years, over 300 shows and worked with two chairmen, Michael Parkinson and Michael Aspel,' he recalls. 'During that spell two boys from Bradford University set up a pop-group called the Lionel Blairs.' Michael's wife Mary would often feature on the women's team as once again the pair showed that they could thrive not just away from the small screen, but also on it. She was always a bright and lively presence on the show and viewers were overjoyed to see the couple's rapport on television again.

Responses to Michael's role on *Give Us A Clue* were widespread. For instance, the *Guardian*'s Jane Ellison wrote: 'Liza Goddard is busy on Thames trying to give Janet and Susan and Jean a clue. And who is this familiar, craggy face above a garishly striped rugby shirt? None other than Michael Parkinson. Rather wearily he hands out his books, films and songs as if remembering the days when he was the prime of Saturday night viewing. Liza Goddard performs a wild pantomime with startling abandon. It emerges that she is trying to mime *The Independence Of Triangles*.' This somewhat cynical view does little justice to the fun that Michael invariably brought to the proceedings. Viewers lapped up every moment of the afternoon's entertainment.

To this day, many recall the show with fond memories. One nostalgic Internet wag wrote: 'There were lots of strange hand gestures to enable you to mime a TV show, book, play, song and so on to the rest of your team in two minutes or less. Holding the requisite number of fingers in the air at the start would tell your team how many words there were in it. Placing the requisite number of fingers on your crooked elbow would tell them how many syllables were in the current word. Putting one finger on your nose and pointing with your other hand would tell the person indicated that they'd guessed correctly – presumably the applause from the audience wasn't enough of a giveaway.

'It was all great fun at the time. And we would diligently look away from the television set when the title was displayed so that we could "play along at home". We would be pleased when familiar faces joined the panels – and we would worry when new faces appeared, concerned that they might not be of the same calibre as the regulars.'

The original theme tune was 'Chicken Man', also used on BBC1's school drama, *Grange Hill*. However, by the time Michael arrived there was a new, catchy and surprisingly long theme tune, which included his name sung out with joy. *Give Us A Clue* has also proved influential. In America, actress Hilary Swank, who won 2005's Best Actress Oscar, developed a television show called *Celebrity Charades*. Broadcast on US cable channel AMC, the show featured two teams of celebrities competing in a game of movie-themed charades. Guests included actors Philip Seymour Hoffman and Hank Azaria, who voices *The Simpsons*.

As well as extensive appearances on television, Michael also continued his writing. The 1980s saw him developing his skill and taking it in an entirely new and somewhat unexpected direction: children's fiction. The stories featured in *The Woofits* concerned a family of anthropomorphic dog-like creatures who lived in the fictional Yorkshire coal-mining village of Grimeworth (based on the real-life Cudworth, where Michael was born, and the nearby village of Grimethorpe). 'They had a very short shelf-life here, but I've since seen unpaid translations in France, Spain, Germany – bloody Woofit books everywhere. They're based on me as a child, in little episodes,' he recalls. 'So is a Woofit a little Parky?' he was asked. 'Mmm... sort of,' was his reply.

Indeed, the appeal was global. In 1983 Michael created a mascot for the Royal Institute for Deaf and Blind Children at North Rocks, Australia, known as 'Rockie Woofit', an Australian version of his UK characters, The Woofits. Although Rockie has since retired from public life, his spirit lives on at the Rockie Woofit Preschool.

This was far from Michael's first venture into publishing. In 1968 he published *Football Daft*. This book is now a rarity, sold only via antiquarian bookstores. Reviews are similarly hard to come by. However, one online shopper has given an eloquent, if at times somewhat eccentric, verdict: 'Michael Parkinson is a brilliant writer and his words will transform your heart. I haven't said this in a while but, "Given the proper permission, I would kiss that man!" And I really haven't said that in a while. He's opened up so many of my eyes towards the bastion majestics of football (or, as the Spanish have it, "Ballet de le fus" – "Feet of the dance!") and I mean, before y'know I would have, "What's an offside?"

but now y'know all is clear. The flowing prose is worth more praise than you'd think. I mean I never knew Parkinson could be such a great writer. But, there are we, a little surprise each day does you goodly.'

Football Daft was followed by *Cricket Mad* in 1969; then in 1977 *Bats In The Pavilion* appeared. The publicity for the latter title had fun with his reputation for being a player of cricket, as well as a reporter of it. 'It took many years for Michael Parkinson's own cricketing exploits to become well-known – the breakthrough came with his appointment as cricket reporter on his local South Yorkshire newspaper. Headlines like "Parkinson Again" or "Another Parkinson Triumph" then became commonplace and even in lean times the readers were guaranteed a "Parkinson Fails" headline every now and again just to keep the name fresh in their minds.

'Parkinson's writing on cricket, as opposed to his performance at the game, was immediately appreciated by the public, and with its special mixture of nostalgia and humour this new part-anthology from Michael Parkinson is as original and witty as its predecessor *Cricket Mad*. Profiles of some of his favourite Yorkshire-born heroes naturally receive an honoured place – including a timely feature on local lad Geoff Boycott – but in *Bats in the Pavilion* the author also produces far-ranging and equally humorous or thought-provoking essays on the game and its characters at every level.

'In his own assessment, all Michael Parkinson's useful knowledge and attitudes to life came from his father. It is a case of like father, like son, and to understand one you have to understand the other. As a regular umpire in home matches at Barnsley his "Old Man" used to leap in the air and join the home bowlers in ear-shattering appeals for lbw, leaving the departing batsmen with serious doubts about his impartiality. Michael Parkinson feels that his own capacity to be objective about the game is the one exception that proves the rule.' *Bats In The Pavilion* was illustrated by Derek Alder of the *Sunday Times* and was full of sharp, but highly entertaining comments on the sport, which at the time of publication suddenly found its feet again.

Away from the publishing world, Michael was ready for his next step in television. However, this was to involve unknown territory for all. On 17 January 1983, the landscape of British television would change dramatically and forever. From now on, as people ate their breakfast and prepared for the day, they had the option of watching TV. Previously, anyone foolish enough to switch on the television set at such an hour was confronted by nothing more entertaining than the Test Card. This would remain the state of affairs until late morning, when the first programmes of the day would be shown. So the launch of breakfast television was a bold one.

Having decided to go down that route, the BBC and ITV were soon racing to be first out of the traps at the breakfast hour. The received wisdom was that ITV would win this 'egg-and-bacon' race. However, it was the BBC who came first, launching *Breakfast Time* on 17 January 1983. It cost a cool £6 million to get the show together and it was the faces of Frank Bough, Selina Scott and Nick Ross that were the

A promotional photograph of Michael Parkinson from the early 1970s.
© Hulton-Deutsch Collection/CORBIS

'I wanted to be a journalist since the age of ten.'

Top left: Michael cut his journalistic teeth on the *Daily Express* and *Manchester Guardian* before moving in to television with a job on current affairs show *Scene at 6.30*.

Top right: Ever comfortable in front of the camera, by the 1970s Michael was making a name for himself as one of Britain's most respected TV and radio presenters.

Bottom: Michael's charm and good manners are praised for putting everyone he works with, from celebrities to schoolchildren, at ease, as this picture from the ITV archive shows.

Modelling a tie from Mary Quant's first men's collection at London's
Savoy Hotel in 1972. © *Hulton-Deutsch Collection/CORBIS*

Top left: Michael and Mary at home with their young family.

Top right: At the *What the Papers Say* Awards in 1968. Michael is shown chatting to television executive David Plowright, who gave him his first break in TV with *Scene at 6.30*.   © *REX Features*

Bottom: Relaxing after the first live broadcast of *TV-am* with (*l-r*) Robert Kee, Angela Rippon, David Frost and Anna Ford.   © *PA Photos*

Top left: George Best was a regular guest on *Parkinson* and became a close friend of Michael's. He wrote a biography of the star and is pictured (*inset*) at Best's 50th birthday celebrations on BBC2.

© *Hulton-Deutsch Collection/CORBIS/PA Photos*

Top right: David Beckham was a guest on the last *Parkinson* show in December 2007, where he spoke to Michael about relinquishing England's captaincy.

© *REX Features*

Bottom: Meeting HRH Queen Elizabeth at a film premiere in 1978. Thirty years later she would present him with his knighthood *(inset)*.

© *REX Features*

Michael's father ensured his son grew up playing and loving cricket.

Top: Michael travelled to Sydney to interview legendary bowler Shane Warne in January 2007. Conversation ranged from his famous spin bowling technique to marital infidelities in what was a record-breaking ratings-winner for the channel.

Inset: Sharing a joke with fellow Yorshireman Michael Vaughan at a charity fundraiser dinner.   © *PA Photos*

Bottom left: Ian Botham talked about the tough decision to choose between professional football and cricket when he appeared on Michael's *One to One* show in the late 1980s.

Bottom right: Michael's respected *On Cricket* book is a collection of his best and wittiest journalism on the sport he still loves to play.

© *REX Features*

Top: Long-term Berkshire resident Michael seen chatting to Reading FC Chairman John Madejski.

© PA Photos

Bottom: Mary Parkinson is often seen partnering Michael at charity golf events.

© REX Features

'Anybody who's been married to a man for forty odd years knows he's all talk!'

Michael and Mary at the 2002 BAFTA television awards.

first to be seen on British television at dawn. The team was completed by Russell Grant, who pitched up to do the horoscopes, Diana Moran, aka 'The Green Goddess', who put the more energetic viewers through a work-out and handsome Francis Wilson, who did the weather forecast and won the hearts of housewives across the nation.

Francis Wilson gives an interesting insight into the somewhat chaotic way his weather forecasts were put together back then: 'When I was first approached, all the doomsayers were telling me: "Who in their right mind would ever watch TV at 6am?" For me, though, it was more a case of: "Why should I get up at 3am?" It was a very difficult and fraught time of day. You can't just phone people up and find out the weather through the usual channels. I set up a little room on the fire escape, where I had teletext printers connected to the UK Met office, which tapped out a series of information, which all appeared on a big toilet roll of info. I'd run up and down the fire escape in between slots to get an update. I remember thinking this was crazy.'

Russell Grant remembers the era more fondly, despite the early starts. 'I used to get in at 2 o'clock in the morning,' he says. 'And we had great celebrity guests – on the very first day it was Harry Secombe – and I would do astrology charts for the likes of Peter Ustinov, Zsa Zsa Gabor and Dolly Parton. They were wonderful times.'

Indeed, wonderful times that everyone at ITV hoped to reproduce with the rival show, *TV-am*, launched a fortnight after *Breakfast TV* on 1 February 1983. For *TV-am*, chief executive Peter Jay put together a team that became known as the 'Famous Five': David Frost, Angela Rippon, Anna Ford, Robert Kee and Michael Parkinson. They were not merely presenters but also shareholders, giving them a real sense of ownership, involvement and motivation. The station's end copyright caption featured an eggcup and every year another eggcup was added. There were 10 on screen by the time *TV-am* ended in 1992. The idea came from the *TV-am* building, in London's Camden Lock, which had a dozen giant eggcups on the roof.

However, all was to run far from smoothly and within six weeks of the show's first episode, Peter Jay was ousted. So, where did it all go so wrong? One commentator said that *TV-am*'s 'starchy, hard-hitting style' was to blame. In its first year, it made just 40 per cent of the budgeted advertising revenue. Within months of the show's launch, Angela Rippon and Anna Ford were sacked. Ford took the news particularly badly and famously had her revenge when she threw a glass of wine over then-executive Jonathan Aitken at a party.

Looking back, this was unsurprisingly a time of bitterness. 'I remember Anna having a huge row because they wanted her to do an item about female circumcision and, quite rightly, she said that's not what people want at 7am but the suits said: "You'll do it,"' recalls Angela Rippon. 'We were breaking barriers, doing something new, making television history, but the people making the decisions weren't being bold enough to strike ahead. It was a shame and it didn't work out well for Anna and I. The dingbats responsible for making the poor decisions were protected and needed someone to carry the can. We were the public sacrifices. Interestingly, they kept all the blokes.'

They might have kept Michael on, but he was outspoken about the culls. 'Obviously it is not the company we founded. I am sad at what has happened. That was the reason given, but no one is going to stop me talking to the press,' he said. 'The entire programme has been a mess-up from start to finish. The problems are about content on the programme, not the presenters. They should look at the content then ask who should be sacked. That's where it should all start, not with the presenters. It's a poor way of repaying Anna and Angela for all their work. It's absurd to get rid of them.'

So, does it still rankle? 'Oh very much so – we lost our nerve,' he recalls. 'We were frightened off. We were shooed off the golden egg, basically. And all we had to do was sit on it and wait. Because we'd been given the right, the licence to exclusively broadcast adverts between 6.30 and 9.30am. How about that for a proposition? And if you couldn't get that right... what the hell.' He shakes his head and says it was an eye-opener: 'Big business. It's a mucky game, that is. What rankles even more, and it's all our fault, is that we should have kept the diaries. David Frost gave me a book at the time, he gave us all books, and mine said, "Michael Parkinson's Account of *TV-am*." And he left it all blank pages. And nobody filled them in!'

Later, the puppet Roland Rat was brought in and became symbolic of the changes that were made to chase viewers. Michael was not particularly impressed with the way his child, *TV-am*, turned out, feeling that the puppet embodied the dumbing-down of the show. 'We could have achieved the same success without going so far downmarket,' he insists. 'They've got David [Frost], but he's tucked away at the weekend, and there is a marked discrepancy between what he does and what is on screen during the rest of the week. They would be wise to hire someone else of his stature.'

In the aftermath of the *TV-am* débâcle, Michael perhaps hit his lowest point. He admits he was very disenchanted and was drinking a fair bit too. 'Having left what was a great job, my first talk show on BBC, to go into what I thought was a better one at *TV-am*, I ended up with egg on my face,' he says. 'It caused me a huge depression. I didn't have a job, I didn't have a TV company; I had nothing. But I am from the Michael Caine school of performing: that is to do every job you can. Some might be terrible but there might be one or two good ones as well.'

Those close to Michael became enormously troubled about him during this period. 'It was the time I was most worried about him,' remembers Dickie Bird. 'None of his friends saw much of him; he got very low about it all. I used to ring him up, and I knew really he'd come good, but I still worried.' His wife Mary was worried too, particularly by the amount of drink he was consuming. One day, she confronted him and told him he was ugly when drunk. 'That stopped me short,' he recalls.

Expanding on this later, he said: 'It was something in me. I think maybe, at that time in my life, in my career I was unhappy. And I did the classic male thing. I like pubs, I've always liked pubs, I still like pubs; I still like drinking... I mean, I don't drink anything like I used to. I mean, at all – I can't, couldn't possibly, I'd be dead. But I enjoyed that period, but then I got depressive and I got bad-tempered, and I got to a point where I didn't know what I was doing. And Mary said to me, women are very clever, aren't they? They hit you, they know exactly which button to press, and she said to me, "You know your problem now, darling?" and I said, "What?" And she said, "You're incredibly unattractive." And I thought, yeah you're right, you're right.

'[She meant] Unattractive as a person... In every way, in every single way, and she was right, she was right. And you need somebody to sort of... then you look at yourself differently. You say why, why would she say that? And then you look at yourself and you see, by Christ she's right. And then, if you've got any sense at all, then you change your life – which I did.'

Looking back, he attempted to dissect what went wrong: 'We thought winning the franchise would be the most difficult part,' he admitted. 'It turned out to be the easiest. David Frost's "United Artists" notion was all very fine, but it was a dream without foundation. Apart from Frost, the people in front of the camera were not business-minded. We were ill-equipped to deal with the likes of Timothy Aitken and Kerry Packer, who came in and did what they were expected to do: make a lot of money.'

Not that everyone has bitter memories of *TV-am* days. Fellow television presenter Ian White of Wakefield has turned into something of an obsessive of the programme. 'I can't explain it. It was just such a pioneer, something that revolutionised television, and it meant so much to me when I was younger and that has stayed with me,' he says. Recalling the dawning of *TV-am* as 'a sudden burst of sunshine', he has turned his garage into nothing short of a shrine. 'When I was younger I wrote to the show all the time and was at the studios several times, and I would just take whatever I was allowed and soon I had quite a lot of stuff,' he shrugs. 'Then staff started sending me things to do with the show and the collection grew and grew. I used to collect things to do with other shows, but I soon realised that *TV-am* was my real passion and I devoted myself to that.

'The neighbours wouldn't know it to look in the house. It's not like the bedroom is a shrine to Mike Morris. But the garage is just chock-full. There are even parts of the old set in there that I rescued from a skip when my spies told me it was in trouble. It joins a big studio table rescued from *TV-am*'s Camden Lock headquarters in London. There's not much I haven't got now. There's a company that owns 10,000 hours of archive footage, but I don't think I'll be trying to get my hands on that. I can't see many people turning up to a party at my place to watch an episode of *TV-am* from 1986, although to me it sounds like a great night.' A television man himself White has presented the BBC's *Look North* programme: 'Now I'm in TV myself it's just such a shame I will never get a chance to work on a show that meant so much to me. I'm not sad enough to have pretended that I was an interviewer on the show, talking into a hairbrush or anything. Honestly, I haven't...' We believe him.

At this point Michael was also presenting *All Star Secrets* on LWT. The show began life as a segment in *Bruce Forsyth's Big Night* in 1980. Based on a 1979 American NBC format by Michael Hill, it was fairly straightforward. From 1984 to 1986 Michael would invite celebrity guests to his studio and they would reveal a previously unknown secret about themselves. It is fair to say that *All Star Secrets* has not gone down in history as one of the more respected television shows of the 1980s. The *Courier Mail* described it as a show in which 'members of the audience were challenged to pick which prominent politician/singer, actor/comedian Uncle Tom Cobley on the panel had (a) left his wife at the altar (screams of laughter) or (b) sunk the *Bismarck* ("Oooooooh!") or (c) been found in the cabbage patch in his or her pyjamas (titter, titter).'

Nevertheless, Michael's charismatic style carried it all and he did an amazing job of presenting the show, with a series of celebrity guests walking through the studio doors to take part. These included Su Pollard, the now-disgraced pop star Gary Glitter, Bernie Clifton and Derek Nimmo. However, the most memorable episode featured the legendarily drunken Oliver Reed. In August 1985, the actor was due to appear at the end of an edition of *All-Star Secrets* to discuss a run-in he once had with boxer Henry Cooper. However, as he waited in his dressing-room, Reed became restless and punched his fist into the dressing-room mirror. He then went on to smash a hole in the wall separating the studio from backstage, much to the shock of the studio audience. When Michael asked how many rounds he would like to go with Cooper, he failed to reply with the scripted line, 'As many as he will buy.' Instead he took an aimless swing at the boxer. 'He was like a hurricane that blew through but did not kill anyone,' remarked one member of the crew.

As the *Independent* reported: 'The *Help Squad* roped in Michael Parkinson and a lot of noisy people who dress up in red and bustle about the country in a flashy red Helpmobile inflicting assistance on harmless objects. Parkinson has described his new venture as a mix between *That's Life!* and *Jim'll Fix It*. The first episode suggested that someone had been rummaging for ideas in *That's Life*'s editorial dustbin. One item had the squad crashing through the undergrowth of an hotel, trapping an unwanted flock of terrified peacocks to a background chorus of voices explaining how the birds really enjoyed it. Another featured a stout lady motorist who had broken down on a lonely country road. Even the dramatised reconstruction of her plight, with passing drivers made to look like inmates on the run from Broadmoor, could not disguise the fact that a kindly motorist had lent her his car phone to summon help.'

Again, this was television's greatest, less still Michael's own finest, hour. Although he did a fantastic job of presenting the programme, there was little disguising the fact that he deserved a bigger stage. And he was soon to get it in the shape of Yorkshire TV chat show *One To One*. Interestingly, when he announced the launch in 1987, Michael claimed this would be his final television work. 'They will be called "Parkinson One To One" and will see me finished with television,' he stated categorically. 'I have been putting it off and putting it off, but this year I am positive about it. I've had a bloody good run in television and I have reached the stage where there is just no amount of money that would get me back into the mainstream.

'There is nothing more desperate than the sight of a 56-year-old man desperately trying to hold on to his career. After March, all that will be left is a weekly column for the London *Daily Mirror* and my publishing interests.' Thankfully, the retirement side of his statement fizzled out, though the launch of his *One To One* shows had run its course. The highest-profile edition saw singer-songwriter Elton John dramatically announce he was still in love with his ex-wife Renate. 'I love her and she still loves me,' he told Michael. 'We are known as the odd couple, which is fair enough because I made a statement in the 1970s that I was bisexual.' Michael disproved his image as a man who ducks the tough questions when he challenged him about the newspaper allegations he was then fighting. 'Was it the case,' asked Michael, 'that there is no smoke without fire?' 'I am going to fight all the allegations,' replied John. 'Hopefully, I will be victorious. If I am not, I will be distraught.'

Once again, Michael was at the forefront of a headline-grabbing interview. His knack of teasing out interesting answers on sensitive topics belies his reputation as a soft hand. The *One To One* series yet again underscored his ability for television interviews. How long would it be before he was restored to his rightful place at the top of the chat-show game? It was not merely an injustice for him to be sidelined to such comparatively small programmes, for the public too it was a disappointment not to have *Parkinson* on their small screens. For the time being, they would have to content themselves with enjoying him on the radio. There, he would anchor perhaps the best-known show in the medium, a tribute to his stature in the television landscape.

7

RADIO TIMES

On a cold winter's night in 1941, an advertising copywriter-turned-actor called Roy Plomley had a bright idea: he thought of a radio show where celebrities were invited on to list the eight songs they would most like to take with them to a desert island. Later, he admitted that as the idea came to him that night, he never expected it to last more than eight seasons, but he had grossly underestimated its appeal. Thus began the life of the longest-running radio music show on the planet.

Plomley himself became the first host when the programme was launched the following year on 29 January 1942. *Desert Island Discs* was an instant hit and has had a raft of memorable guests through its doors. For instance, comedian Norman Wisdom and pianist Moura Lympany filled their lists with their own recordings. Controversy ensued over the selections of John Major and Jeffrey Archer rumoured to have been made by their advisers. Then there were the somewhat bizarre selections of actor Herbert Lom, who chose a recording of a lengthy standing ovation, and Dame Edith Evans, who requested the whip-cracking theme from *Rawhide*.

One guest, whose identity was never revealed by the team, admitted on arrival at the studio to being tone-deaf and unable to pick a single record. Plomley therefore broke his strict rule of not influencing his guest's choice. Discovering the writer was a passionate dancer he asked him to name his favourite dances and requested researchers to find pleasant examples of them. Then there was a hilarious misunderstanding during Brigitte Bardot's show. She was asked which item she would take to the desert island along with the songs. 'A peeenissss,' she seemed to reply. Plomley asked: 'Most interesting, and why precisely, may I ask?' 'Well,' said Bardot, 'it's what the world needs most, isn't it? 'Appiness.'

By the time Plomley died in 1985, the show had become nothing short of a national institution. On a personal level, he had created for himself the reputation of a fine interviewer. He never interrupted guests and was also noted for the depth of research he undertook. Many held that his replacement would have a major task on their hands. Not that everyone had been a complete fan of his presentation style. 'People used to say that Roy was good at drawing people out,' said Derek Drescher, who was producing the programme at the time. 'But he wasn't. If somebody wasn't talking, he was lost.' Plomely's wife still holds rights to the programme.

So, who would bravely step up to the plate to fill Plomley's shoes? Step forward, Michael Parkinson. He was selected by Diana, Plomley's widow, and Mr David Hatch, controller of Radio 4. Several other names were considered, including Sir John Mortimer, barrister, dramatist and author, and Richard Baker, the former BBC newscaster. Plomley had asked for his widow to be involved in the choice of any successor, so presumably she was happy with Michael's selection, or at least so initially.

Michael seemed more than happy with his new job, as he told reporters: 'I am delighted to be taking over from Roy Plomley. *Desert Island Discs* is one of the more prestigious programmes and I hope I will be able to do it as well and as long as he did.' Naturally, the press asked him how much money he would be paid for his new slot. 'Enough,' he replied, with typical Parky reserve. 'It is not really a question of money in a situation like this. You are looking at one of the plum jobs in radio.' Once he was in the hot seat, he brought in plenty of sporting guests, but subsequent accusations that he only ever invited characters from the sporting world are a little unfair. For instance, he once had fashion designer Bruce Oldfield on the show and memorably asked his guest if he considered 'making frocks was a proper job for a man'. During her appearance on *Desert Island Discs*, actress Stephanie Beachum revealed she is deaf in one ear. 'If I was always skipping to the right of Charlton Heston in *The Colbys* it was just so I could keep up with the dialogue,' she told Michael.

After three years at the helm, Parky announced he was

leaving for pastures new. During his time on the show he faced inexplicable criticism from some quarters. One commentator was confused: 'Why is this odd little radio record programme so important? Why have 70 people applied to present it? Why has Michael Parkinson been under constant attack ever since he took on the job two years ago? Why is it that revealing your banal musical tastes on this quaint little show has become an honour quite as great as an OBE? What exactly is all the fuss about?' Harsh words, perhaps, but the message was reasonable in as much as it applied to Parkinson. No matter what anyone's opinion of his performance, the criticism he now faced seemed disproportionate, to say the least.

And the fuss continued even after he had announced his decision to move on. 'I told the BBC when I took the job that I would only stay for a couple of years,' he told reporters. 'I never regarded *Desert Island Discs* as a pensionable occupation. It was Roy Plomley's genius to invent the format of the programme. It is so perfect that the only way to change the show is to change the presenter.' A BBC spokesman was quick to dispel rumours that there was any animosity: 'It is a perfectly amicable parting on both sides.' However, the storm was about to begin.

Plomley's widow Diana was the first to complain. Speaking of Michael's tenure on the show, she was extremely disparaging, particularly over his choice of guests. 'The guests all seemed to be footballers and cricketers. They tended to be from poor backgrounds and they all harped on about it. There were very few who could be described as intellectual,' she said. Later, she was only marginally less unkind: 'I don't bear him [Parkinson] any rancour. I haven't spoken to anyone about him for five years. I merely think he had the wrong sort of voice and the wrong personality. Events did rather prove me right.' Before long, the pair traded insults with Diana describing Michael as 'an ignorant Yorkshireman' and he described the show created by her husband as 'a silly little programme'. Later, when asked about the falling-out, Michael said simply that she is 'a very easy woman to fall out with.'

In subsequent years, sympathy for him has grown. No longer is he widely seen as the man who failed. Instead people credit him for his efforts and recognise how difficult it was to step into the shoes of the show's creator and first presenter. For instance, Michael's own successor, Sue Lawley, had both sympathy and gratitude for him. 'I realised within the first year of doing *Desert Island Discs* that this could be the beginning of something new and that it was working for me,' she said. 'It was going to be okay so I could use it as the new cornerstone of my career. Because of *Desert Island Discs*, I have been able to carve out a new existence for myself which was different to what I now regard in hindsight as the treadmill one that I had before.' She added: 'The truth is that the problems Michael Parkinson had made it easier for me because all I had to do was to put it back to where it was. It was harder for Parky because he was stepping into Roy Plomley's shoes.'

His next job in radio was a notably different affair and a far less rancorous one. Even there, though, he experienced brushes with controversy. Billed as 'an entertaining, engrossing and intelligent conversation between the presenters and the listeners, covering the thoughts and topics that Londoners are really talking about,' LBC has had an eventful history. It began broadcasting in October 1973, a week prior to the launch of Capital Radio and kicked off with the words: 'This is London Broadcasting, the news and information voice of independent radio' voiced by David Jessell. As his colleague, Ken Guy, explained, the opening day was, in many ways, eventful: 'The first announcer that morning was David Jessel who, I'm told, was physically ill into the wastepaper basket in his studio,' he recalls, adding: 'Fortunately I was in the other main studio.

'We went on air in the middle of the Yom Kippur war, a marvellous coincidence for us at LBC, not so great for the combatants. I still have a tape of the first hour, complete with messages from Harold Wilson and Edward Heath. I also brought back to Brisbane press clippings of LBC's first year, with all its ups and downs. Some of the headlines were shockers for those who worked there. I also have Fleet Street cartoons lampooning my Aussie accent and original news copy, which us readers were expected to read on air word perfect.'

In many ways, this was one of the first examples of a rolling news radio station in the UK. One of the earliest presenter pairings was Janet Street-Porter and Paul Callan on the breakfast show. The pair frequently clashed on-air and for many Londoners, it became required listening. Other presenters in those early years included Jon Snow, Carol

Barnes, Julian Manyon, Dennis Rookard, George Gale, Mike Field, Brian Hayes, Peter Simpson and Julian Bray. However, LBC was beset with problems and in 1994 spokesman James Worsley announced: 'We can confirm as a matter of public record that administrative receivers were appointed late last night.' It came down to Reuters to save the day, with the company taking over until 1996.

But this was after Michael joined the ranks. In 1990, he came on board to present the *Michael Parkinson Show*, which went out in the morning and attracted around 750,000 listeners. The job involved early mornings, but he was compensated for these with a reported annual salary of £110,000 for presenting the show, which naturally had plenty of memorable moments. One of the earliest was the time when Lady Olga Maitland criticised people on social security and was challenged by Michael to live it as she talked it. So it was that Olga Maitland handed over her cash and credit cards to him and began a week of enforced poverty, moving into a London Council Bed and Breakfast to live on £4.13 a day. 'It's going to be highly educational,' she said. 'I want to learn about this first-hand.' She gave daily reports of her experiences to Michael's show.

However, the most newsworthy incident that happened during his LBC years was undoubtedly the time when he lost his patience with a caller, landing himself in hot water in the process. During a show in November 1991, a Canadian caller complained about life in England and the Gulf War. Michael's normally calm and collected patience finally snapped and he told the caller: 'If you think it's so bloody awful, why don't you sod off?' Perhaps not an unreasonable sentiment, but the delivery was a little blunt. Naturally, some listeners took offence and complained to both the station and to the Radio Authority. The latter body ultimately upheld complaints on the incident and issued a stern warning to the station. Michael was later forced to apologise on air.

Further scrutiny was to come. Another regulatory body, the Broadcasting Standards Council, adjudicated on two further incidents on the show at which listeners said they had taken offence. In one, in which a listener complained that extracts featuring child abuse were read out from a book about the Marquis de Sade, the Broadcasting Standards Council judged the subject had been dealt with in 'a proper and serious manner'. In the other, a discussion of a recent 'outing' of a gay man, a listener said Parkinson used the word 'Nancy' to describe homosexuality. The complaint was not upheld because the Broadcasting Standards Council accepted LBC's response that the word was not used, but was a mishearing of the words 'was' and 'is'.

He was not the only LBC presenter to fall foul of the radio authorities that year. Mike Carlton, presenter of the station's 'drive-time' show, brushed aside on-air confusion as to the location of the station's European correspondent by joking that it 'doesn't matter at all out there – wogs begin at Calais.' The Radio Authority also ruled that a satirical song on Steve Jones' breakfast show about whether single women should have children by artificial insemination 'could have caused some distress to listeners with deeply held Christian beliefs'. As for

Michael, he remained polite and philosophical in the face of all this. Ever the professional broadcaster, he is all for regulatory bodies in broadcasting. 'You can't have media without some checks or it's total anarchy,' he shrugged. He did add, though, that the people who staff regulatory bodies, such as the Broadcasting Standards Council, sometimes lack the relevant experience to adjudicate on such matters. 'They don't know what it is like to be live on air, responding to viewers' opinions and prejudices, for three hours a day,' he said.

Turning to the incident in question, he admitted: 'I lost my temper with a listener, which is perfectly normal, and I have to learn to be more temperate but language does not matter any more anyway. Who has ever died of a four-letter word on the radio? Who will faint at hearing "Sod off"? The real issues are to do with attitudes such as racism. We do need a checkpoint, a higher authority, but they need to be a damn sight more sophisticated in their approach to complaints than they are at present.' Sophisticated or not, the regulators had done the job they intended to do in his case because Michael admitted their warning had made him more wary of straying over the line in future. 'The trouble with a rebuke,' he said, 'is that one is immediately aware of being much more cautious, which I suppose is the intention.'

It was viewers who took offence to that episode, though, when the tables turned as a result of one LBC incident which had him as the one taking umbrage at something someone said. In June 1992, as bids flew around, a rival consortium held talks with the radio authority about taking over LBC. Were they to succeed, they said, they would seek to keep

Michael on. But their words fell on ungrateful ears: 'I got pretty angry when I heard them say that. They are not talking about the office junior,' he said. 'In fact, I would never work for them and I don't need to be told their views about broadcasting. But what really annoys me is people making assumptions on my behalf.'

When the news broke that his producer Jo Phillips had been selected as Liberal Democrat candidate for Thanet North, this time assumptions were made by the Conservative Party. 'LBC has always been more anti-Tory than the BBC,' said one unnamed Tory MP. Phillips, who abandoned the studio when the election was called, insisted that she remained completely impartial in her LBC work. 'I am quite able to separate my private and work lives,' she said. 'It's not as if I am a member of the militant socialists or the National Front.'

During LBC days, the Conservative Party was at the centre of one of the biggest scoops of Michael's career. When he was at Granada, Parkinson worked on the show that first broke the news that President John F. Kennedy had been shot. In 1991, he was at the station that was the first to announce that Prime Minister Margaret Thatcher had resigned, only this time, Michael was the man with the scoop, beating Radio 4 by 11 minutes.

In later years, his son Andrew worked at LBC and it was during his tenure there that he himself hit the headlines when it was revealed that he had once dated Prince Edward's fiancée, Sophie Rhys-Jones. 'Yes, it's true, I did briefly go out with her,' said Andrew, then sports editor at

LBC, whose wife Debbie also worked at Capital as the managing director's PA. 'I got the shock of my life when I picked up the newspapers today. I knew nothing about it [the engagement]. I only saw her two weeks ago and she was the soul of discretion. If it's true then I'm very pleased for her. She's lovely, very bubbly, great fun to be with. But ours was never really a serious relationship. We only went out for a few weeks and had a few laughs. I wish her all the luck in the world.' Michael said at the time that he was very proud of his son.

But Parkinson was losing interest in LBC and this was mainly because of the shockingly early rises he had to make to get to the studio on time. Getting up at 5am, he said, made him feel as if he had 'permanent jet-lag'.

Halloween is supposed to be an eventful, sometimes slightly scary time of year. But the Halloween of 1992 was destined to be a little different to any other that Michael Parkinson – and BBC viewers – had ever witnessed before. He had never been one to find himself at the centre of controversy to any noticeable extent, preferring to make headlines for the best of reasons. From his journalism at the *Daily Express* during the 1960s and the *Manchester Guardian*, to his mammoth success in the broadcasting arena, he had written and talked about controversial incidents in other people's lives on a regular basis. Never had he been involved in such trouble himself. However, with a career in the frontline of broadcasting, he was eventually to become caught up in a troublesome project.

That project turned out to be the drama *Ghostwatch*. Written by Stephen Volk and produced by Ruth Baumgarten, the 90-minute film was a horror story shot in a documentary style. It was part of BBC Drama's 'Screen One' series. Appearing as a live cross between *Crimewatch* and the movie *Poltergeist*, in *Ghostwatch* Michael joined other familiar television faces Sarah Greene, Craig Charles and Mike Smith to investigate reports of a ghost named Pipes, who was disturbing a family called the Earlys, who lived in Northolt, London. The family clamed poltergeist activity had been going on at their home.

The 1989 show featured evidence that a ghost had been knocking on the plumbing of the Early's house, thus giving it the nickname 'Pipes'. Then, later in the programme, viewers were told that Pipes was the spirit of a psychologically disturbed man called Raymond Tunstill, thought to have been troubled by the spirit of a child-killer from the nineteent century. *Ghostwatch* becomes more and more terrifying until, at the conclusion, the frightened reporters realised that the programme itself was acting as a sort of 'national séance' through which 'Pipes' was gaining even greater and more terrifying power. Finally, the spirit escaped and began to escalate its poltergeist activity in the BBC studios themselves, possessing Michael as a prelude to its unleashing on the world.

In the twenty-first century the viewing public are more savvy to television hoaxes and 'mockumentaries'. In *Space Cadets* three reality TV contestants are duped by Johnny Vaughan into thinking they are being taken to space. Dramas such as *The Office* blur the line between documentary and fiction. Also, there are hoax television interviews such as those performed by comic acts like Ali G and Chris Morris: we are well-versed in the fact that television occasionally plays tricks on those participating in shows, and on us, the viewers. However, the early 1990s was a comparatively innocent time. This was prior to the explosion of the Internet and of cable and satellite TV. Therefore, viewers were far more likely to take what they saw on television as gospel, particularly anything shown on the BBC. Throw into the mix the fact that Michael, a trusted and loved institution, was taking part and it becomes less surprising to learn that *Ghostwatch* caused panic across the nation.

As writer Stephen Volk says, 'It's quite difficult now to think back to the televisual landscape of 1992. Formats that dissolve the boundaries between factual and fictional TV have since become the staple diet of the schedules and it's difficult to imagine a world where they were new or unusual. But this was the time of the first successful hybrids: docu-dramas and drama-docs. Drama series like *NYPD Blue* increasingly employed a hand-held camera style derived from documentary realism, and documentaries like *Crimewatch* and *999* were full of reconstructions using actors mix-and-matched to real footage of real people.'

Certain realistic elements added to the sense of authenticity. A phone number featured on the screen so that viewers could call in and discuss the ghostly goings-on. The telephone number was the normal BBC call-in number, also used on other Beeb shows such as *Going Live!* Those callers who got through to the line were initially connected to a message telling them that the show was fictional. They were then given the chance to share their own ghost stories with switchboard operators.

Added to the confusion was the set, which appeared to be a normal BBC documentary one. Moreover, the filming methods used for *Ghostwatch*, including shaky hand-held video cameras, lent much to the documentary feel. On a number of occasions during the programme, Michael and the other presenters examined video footage of a bedroom in the Early's house. There, a sinister and shadowy figure is seen at the foot of a child's bed. Three versions of the apparition are shown intermittently to confuse the viewer – one with the figure, one where it is slightly faded out, and one in which it is absent altogether.

The ghost is a disfigured man in a dark robe. He appears in the studio set and outdoor scenes too, sometimes very subtly or subliminally. When Charles is interviewing various Northolt folk, the ghost can be seen standing, unnoticed, among the crowd of onlookers. As a tape of a possessed voice is played in the studio, one can see the ghost again, particularly if the brightness of the screen is increased.

In *Ghostwatch* it is claimed that many characters are possessed by a ghost: this possession shows itself in people when they begin to bizarrely recite nursery rhymes as the sound of cats in pain is heard in the background. The eldest daughter of the Early family is one example, but so too is Michael himself who, towards the end of the programme, appears possessed. 'Up and down the garden path,' he recites, as his voice distorts and a cat is heard screaming.

Ghostwatch was clearly influenced in part by the US radio show *The War Of The Worlds*. The first half was presented as a series of news bulletins, in which it was claimed that a genuine alien invasion was in progress. There was public outcry against the episode, but director Orson Welles was launched to huge fame in the process. Newspaper reports claimed panic erupted among viewers who took the news bulletins at face value. People were said to be fleeing the area and others claimed they could smell poison gas, or could see the flashes of the lightning in the distance. Studies estimate 6 million heard the broadcast, with 1.7 million believing it was true. Most were found to be 'genuinely frightened'.

The panic that greeted *Ghostwatch* was not quite so severe but it still resulted in the BBC being bombarded with phone calls from terrified or angry viewers. As the *Sunday Times* reported the following morning: 'The BBC was swamped with complaints last night from viewers terrified by a Hallowe'en television drama which appeared to be all too realistic. The switchboard at the corporation's television centre in west London was jammed for more than an hour after the fictional 90-minute *Ghostwatch* drama ended.' A BBC worker was quoted as saying: 'People have been terribly upset by the programme and the fact that it was not broadcast that it was a drama. People thought it was real.' Scotland Yard confirmed police in London had received several calls from people who were worried by the programme. A spokesman said: 'All callers were reassured that the programme was fictitious and that there was no need for any police action.'

The show gained worldwide notoriety, with the *South*

China Morning Post reporting: 'A Halloween TV special was so realistic that thousands of viewers rang the BBC in panic. *Ghostwatch* featured a fictional investigation by a BBC team of journalists at Britain's "most haunted house". Michael Parkinson played the anchorman of a "watchdog"-style current affairs programme.' Meanwhile, over in Australia: TV SHOW SPOOKS BRITISH VIEWERS screamed the *Herald Sun* headline.

One of the viewers to complain was John Turvey from North London. 'I was terrified,' he remembers. 'They really had me fooled by the phone-in. And I was in a right state when they showed the girl covered in blood and disfigured.' His fears were shared by Nicole Murcott from Essex: 'With Michael Parkinson presenting the thing, I believed it was real.' In Northolt, people begged the police to help the fictitious family. 'We had lots of calls from some very upset and worried people but we managed to convince them that it was only pretend,' said a spokesman.

Closer to home, friends reportedly phoned Michael's wife Mary to make sure that he was okay, following his ghostly scene. 'As cameramen collapsed and scratches appeared on a girl's face, friends of Parkinson were so concerned that they called his wife Mary to ensure she was safe,' claimed Rebecca Hardy in the *Daily Mail*. He himself shrugged off the controversy. 'It just shows what a capacity television has for delusion,' he said. 'I have no concerns whatsoever about the show. It was designed to frighten people, not to make them sit back in their armchairs and laugh. It was clearly billed as a drama in the *Radio Times*.

'You always get a certain percentage who believe everything on television is real. Some people even believe all-in wrestling is for real. The great majority of people who watched that programme would have realised it was a drama. But if it does for my career what it did for Orson Welles' career, I shall be delighted.'

The alarm that followed *Ghostwatch* was soon to take a tragic turn for the worst, however. Martin Denham was 18 when he watched the show and soon after he committed suicide. As his parents tried to come to terms with their shock and grief, they pointed the finger of blame squarely at the programme. Mrs Denham, 41, said: 'This programme killed my dear son. Michael Parkinson and the BBC will have his death on their consciences. Michael Parkinson said later anyone who believed it must have been living under a stone for the past few weeks. Well, my boy believed it and he took his life because of it. Martin had watched horror films without being frightened,' said the mother-of-four. 'He knew the difference between reality and fantasy, but this was so real.'

'On Sunday he didn't eat his lunch, which was not like him,' said his 51-year-old father. 'He was stopping friends and neighbours in the street, asking about the programme and ghosts. On Tuesday he started on about ghosts again, even asking if there was one in our house,' he continues. 'I laughingly told him there must be a ghost in this place because all the biscuits keep disappearing. It was meant as a joke, the lads just help themselves. But Martin just went quiet.' The next morning he was found hanged by a length of nylon hosepipe from the Witch Tree – killed by asphyxia, said a pathologist at the inquest opened and adjourned in Nottingham on the Friday.

The alleged *Ghostwatch* connection was made by Denham's family following their son's suicide note, which read: 'Dear Mam, please don't worry: if there are ghosts I will be a ghost and I will be with you always as a ghost.' A BBC spokesman said: 'Of course, we are very sorry to hear of this tragic event. However, we need to know more about this case before venturing any comment.' Parkinson added: 'It is a terrible tragedy for the family and I do not want to add to their misery.' Supportive as ever, Mary added: 'It is awful and tragic, and Michael is very sorry for the family. But I don't think you can expect him to regret having done it, that's ridiculous. It was billed as a drama, although a lot of my friends were taken in by it, too.'

Writer Stephen Volk remains proud of his work. He says that when he first created the script, he did not have Michael specifically in mind for a part. However, he did plan for the presenter roles to be filled by famous and suitable faces. 'It was written with Presenter, Female Reporter, Phone-In Presenter in the script, but with a note on the cover saying these would be real TV presenters,' he says. 'It made for a clumsy read but I got tired of taking out Jonathan Dimbleby and putting in John Humphrys or Anneka Rice (who I seem to remember turned it down, by the way!) and every change of name affected the way you read the programme.'

Volk, who also wrote Ken Russell's *Gothic*, scripts for the BBC's *Ghosts* and Channel 4's *Shockers*, as well as BAFTA-winning short *The Deadness of Dad* and others, adds: 'We wanted Nick Ross but the Powers That Be said, "No way!" Luckily Sarah Greene trained as an actress – we were lucky there – and her experience of live TV was invaluable. She was offered it and showed it to hubbie Mike Smith, and he wanted to be in it too. A colleague phoned me and said: "What do you think, the two of them in it, one in the studio, one in the house?" And after about two seconds I said, "Fantastic!" So I reshaped the script to reflect the husband-wife thing.

'Sarah's story about seeing the ghost was true, by the way – I was all for that. Craig Charles was a great choice and I think re-did his lines pretty much, which is great. I said to Michael Parkinson (who loved the script and got it completely): "Look, you've been doing this lark for 25 years, if it doesn't sound right, do what does sound right!" and he was fantastic, absolutely a brilliant anchor for the show.'

As well as acknowledging Michael's brilliant acting in the show, Volk also agrees that he was a key factor in giving the whole thing punch and authority: 'It was weird to be accosted by a lady in a shop the next day who said, "'Ere! My young lad was awake all last night because of you! We had to take down his luminous skeleton off the back of his bedroom door!" (To which one might say: what was the skeleton doing on his door in the first place?)

'I was also amazed that a friend of mine, whom I had told to watch out for this programme "wot I wrote", phoned me to say she had believed it totally. I said, "But I told you, I wrote it." She said, "I know, but as soon as I saw Michael Parkinson I thought you must have got it wrong!"'

The *Guardian*'s Nancy Banks-Smith came up with some witty praise: 'You might say *Ghostwatch* was a trick and a treat. Sarah Greene, all of a-twitter, flitted around like a bat in a bow. Craig Charles, cast as the poor devil who is always stuck outside in the cold, interviewed Arthur, an unsuccessful exorcist in his spare time from British Rail. Mike Parkinson twiddled his sceptical spectacles with the air of a man who knows where he can get posh designer frames for half the price.'

To this day, *Ghostwatch* remains a cult classic. In some nostalgic articles on the BBC website, looking back at the show, one wag commented: 'I watched *Ghostwatch* on a dark, wet night with a friend and two bottles of wine. We started off with the lights off. After half an hour, the lights were firmly back on, most of the wine was gone and we were huddled together whimpering on the sofa.

'*Ghostwatch* is deceptive. The first few minutes are convincingly tedious: the hilariously cheesy set with fake fireplace, the crushingly over-sensitive expert with lovely legs, and Michael Parkinson's "Why-am-I-taking-this-so-seriously?" expression. Then it starts to get stranger and stranger, and you start to get truly, truly scared. Even though you know it's not real, you take it all the more seriously because it looks and behaves just like bland factual television.'

Another nostalgic commented: '*Ghostwatch* really should be better remembered than reviewed but if anything it's scarier, craftier, and smarter the second time around. Such a shame, as it may never be broadcast again. It is easy to see why many viewers fell for it. Though some of the actors aren't up to the job of "being real", the presenters excel at playing themselves. The visuals are devilishly trick or treat, either slight of hand or heart-stopping glimpses of the supernatural.'

He added that he would like to see a repeat of the show, arguing it might help heal public feelings: 'What does amaze, though, is that no one saw through the over-the-top ending. "We've created a national seance?" I mean, really! Magicians say people don't mind being tricked, so long as they have a chance to appreciate how clever the con was. Why not give the public another chance to see how ingenious *Ghostwatch* really was?'

The BBC eventually banned the programme, but a DVD release is available. Also, it has been shown in other parts of the world, including Canada, where one TV critic described it as 'a real humdinger'.

In 1995 Michael was at the helm of the revival of a TV show from yesteryear. *Going for a Song* had been a hit for the BBC between 1965 and 1977 and in 1995 the Beeb decided to resurrect it for a new audience. The press greeted the news that Michael was to be the presenter of the all-new *Going for a Song* rapturously. PARKY'S ON SONG FOR HIS TV RETURN beamed the *Evening Standard*. PARKINSON IS THE MAN ON SONG chimed the *Glasgow Herald*. PARKINSON DUSTS OFF THE BIRD FOR MATCH MADE IN BBC HEAVEN enthused the *Guardian*, while the *Daily Mail* went with PARKY'S GOING FOR AN ENCORE.

In the *Guardian* Edward Pilkington wrote an enthusiastic article announcing: 'Two of the great names in television history – *Going for a Song* and Michael Parkinson – are to be pulled off the shelf and relaunched with a new shine. The match, announced yesterday by the BBC, could be one made in heaven. Both were groundbreakers. The antiques programme was one of the most successful game-shows during its 12-year run until 1977. Mr Parkinson was definitive as a chat-show host from 1971 to 1982. The revamped *Going for a Song* is likely to be less reverential towards inanimate old objects than the original was. While it may not be the most exciting job in television, at least Mr Parkinson, aged 60, can draw encouragement from his predecessor. *Going for a Song* propelled its resident expert, the late Arthur Negus, from a nonentity into a media star, aged 61.'

Michael of course was already famous, but this did not prevent his ever-enthusiastic nature from bubbling to the surface as he discussed his new job: 'I know next to nothing about antiques, but it doesn't matter – I'm just a presenter. The programme isn't in that protected haven in the schedules where you know you're going to get viewers: it's on at lunchtime. Therefore it has to work a lot harder to get an audience and it has certainly done much better than I would have thought.'

After the first show went out, the critics were impressed by the new version, as well as Michael's part in it. Peter Paterson of the *Daily Mail* wrote: 'Nearly 20 years ago *Going for a Song* went to the great antique store in the sky. Yesterday, it was reincarnated under the chairmanship of Michael Parkinson and didn't show its age a bit.' Yet again,

Parky had turned his hand to a new television challenge and passed the test with flying colours.

Going for a Song became a highly entertaining show for all manner of reasons. Competition between team captains Mariella Frostrup and Helen Lederer became so fierce that host Michael was at one point forced to step in and remind them that it was just a game-show. 'It was like refereeing the World Cup because there was so much competition,' he quipped. But there was more horror than laughter when Tony Slattery accidentally broke a figurine brought in by a guest. The owner of the £1,000 piece watched in horror from the studio audience as the presenter stood, speechless at his mistake. To make matters worse, the figurine was one of a pair of nineteenth-century Samson models, which together are valued at three times their individual worth. Slattery's slip during the recording in Birmingham was edited out when the show was broadcast and the BBC compensated the owner.

While promoting *Going for a Song*, Michael had a pop at generously paid American chat-show hosts such as David Letterman. 'The BBC flew him over here from America and he stood there looking like he could have been from Mars,' he stormed. 'He is not an interviewer, he is a stand-up performer, and the guests he has on become stooges in his act. He was allowed to get away with a very lazy performance by the BBC. It was c***.'

Meanwhile, *Going for a Song* was a huge success and viewers lapped up every episode. As the pre-recorded episodes were broadcast, Michael was enjoying the

Australian sunshine in Sydney with his wife, visiting his new grandson James. But he was soon back in the UK to present an historical and legendary evening in British broadcasting history, hosting the BBC's evening *Auntie's All Time Greats*. The two-hour extravaganza was part of the corporation's 'TV60' celebrations. It was a glittering affair, attended by the great and the good of British television. As BBC chief executive Will Wyatt accurately quipped: 'It is an amazing night. If a bomb dropped on the building, there would not have been a broadcasting industry tomorrow. We've seen a wonderful array of talent.'

The evening was watched by 12.5 million viewers and kicked off with a message of support from then Prime Minister Tony Blair. 'Everywhere you go in the world, people talk about the BBC and what it stands for,' he said. 'First it's high quality – everyone associates the BBC with really high-quality programmes, and second, it's part of the public service broadcasting that really matters to people.' He added that the BBC was: 'an institution in the United Kingdom. We have grown up with it – it's hard to imagine what daily life would be without the BBC. We turn to it for great State occasions, we turn to it for the news; we turn to it for entertainment. It is an ever-present part of our lives.'

With such glowing words setting the scene for an extraordinary night, it was time for Michael to start handing out the awards. Already he had made it clear who he hoped he would be favouring: 'If I had to pick one BBC programme, it would be any *Morecambe and Wise* show. They have given me more pleasure than anyone else.' In conclusion, he joked: 'If they don't win at least two awards, I'll walk off stage.' Happily, not just for Michael but for everyone involved, he was not forced to see his joke threat through for the *Morecambe And Wise* Show won two gongs on the night: Best Light Entertainment Show and Favourite Performers.

Ernie Wise and Eric Morecambe's widow Joan collected the two trophies. Wise, then 70, said: 'I wish Eric had been with me, the two of us would have been marvellous. The show is popular because it's what the public still like.' Mrs Morecambe, whose husband died 12 years prior to the extravaganza, said: 'We miss him all the time. I don't think a day goes by when his name doesn't crop up. The whole family miss him.' She added: 'He would have been absolutely thrilled by the award and the only sad thing about it is that he isn't here.'

Another award that would have particularly thrilled Michael was Ronnie Barker's prize for Outstanding Achievement. The star of *Porridge* and *Open All Hours* said: 'I haven't done a stroke of work for nine years. A lot of people don't know I've retired because of repeats. I don't miss television at all – I quit while I was ahead. I've been offered stuff, but I always turn it down.' He was, at the time, running an antique shop in Chipping Norton, Oxfordshire. His down-to-earth response to his fame must have chimed with Michael's own relaxed nature.

It was a busy night. Michael also handed over awards to David Jason (Sitcom Performer), the stars of *Men Behaving Badly* (Sitcom), Victoria Wood (Comedy Series and Comedy

Performer), Colin Firth (Actor), Patricia Routledge (Actress), *Dr Who* (Popular Drama) and *Pride And Prejudice* (Drama Serial). Des Lynam received a Sports Presenter award. Sports fan and host Michael made a point of making a statement about the corporation's coverage of sport and its future: 'Sport is one area where the BBC's excellence has been challenged by money. It is very difficult to see the BBC recovering from that. But in other areas it is unchallenged. It is not just that the BBC is the best, it is incomparably the best, and there is nothing within spitting distance of it. It is not a question of whether the BBC can flourish: it *has* to.' It was a sentiment shared by everyone present that night.

The handing over of trophies must have been an enjoyable evening for Michael, who has always been a generous man. If, however, he did at any point feel some jealousy with those who were showered by prizes and praise, he would soon overcome it as he himself was about to become the recipient of honour after gong, after trophy after prize.

8

GONGS GALORE!

In 1998, Michael finally returned to our screens where we wanted him to be: on *Parkinson*. During its first run, the show had been regularly watched by as many as 12 million viewers with up to 17 million tuning in at peak times. Therefore, there was joy in living rooms across the land when the new series was announced. For the past three years, the BBC had been re-running old editions and it seemed those golden memories had led to the corporation's decision to bring *Parkinson* back.

The press, too, were delighted to see him back and ran large interviews and profiles celebrating his return. Vicki Woods, writing in the *Observer*, captured a quirky image of his charm as a chat-show host, by looking back at his form during the first run of *Parkinson*. 'His body language was always fantastically natural,' she wrote. 'Not what you'd call relaxed: he hunched in his seat, screwed his eyes up and famously scratched his nose and his ear and his head throughout the programme (these last all presumably body language for Help! Boring! Time for a laugh! Ask another question!). When his guests said something funny, he flung his head back, kicked his legs out and shouted Har! Har! Har! which got the audience falling off their seats as well.' Though comfortable with sports stars, whom he adored, Woods thought that Michael's years on *Cinema* prepared him amply for his encounters with 'the serene old highnesses from the Hollywood studio system. He was good, if occasionally squirmy, with sexy young women. He was thrown, sometimes, by guests who were too stoned or drunk to be funny, though I'd happily watch George Best from intensive care at the Minnesota Clinic, myself. He never did many politicians (though there was one sticky encounter with Enoch Powell, whose ferocious intellect seemed to throw Parky off-balance and I thought I saw real terror in his eyes). Wasn't he keen to do more politicians? "No." Wouldn't he like to do Lady Thatcher? "No, I wouldn't like to do her. And I wouldn't like to interview her either." Boom! Boom!'

Michael was now 62 years of age and he told interviewers that he was a 'different person, different time, different hair, different neck sizes'. Nonetheless, he was held up as an example of a golden age and was happy with this state of affairs. 'I think that works in your favour,' he said. He then showed how he had grown and matured as an interviewer and a person since the last time *Parkinson* filled the airwaves. 'I remember I used to call everybody "Mr" or "Mrs" or "Miss". Halfway through the interview with Orson Welles he said, "Call me Orson," and I said, "I prefer Mr Welles," and he said, "Why?" and I said something appallingly pompous like, "Out of deference to your stature," and he said, "Bullshit!" So I called him "Orson" from that point on.'

Indeed, his experience and advanced age turned out to be an advantage, he found: 'In those days I suppose I was overawed by them. But really in a talk show, the guests become more conversational and more relaxed if they think they already know you. I watched Robin Williams and Billy Crystal on the *Oprah Winfrey Show* yesterday and they were fantastic, wonderful, because they treated her as someone of equal stature. She got a performance from them they wouldn't give to anyone else.'

Mindful that in the youth-oriented age of the late twentieth century some would mock him, he had a jokey idea for the beginning of his first show back: 'I wanted to make a grand entrance on a chair lift, with a shawl draped round my shoulders,' he smiled. 'After all, I am 62 and it is more than 15 years since I last did a show like this. But I do think that as I have got older, I have got better at interviewing – it is something that improves with age.'

As ever, he applied a straightforward test to any potential guests. 'I am still interested in the same people I had on the shows before – it's just that a lot of them are dead,' he giggled. 'I am interested in anyone who has talent, no matter what age they are, and we have had no problem at all getting guests. The only test I have ever applied to guests is not, do I like them? Or even, do I admire them? But, am I interested in them enough to do an interview? His quip that many of the guests he was interested in having on the show were now dead also had a flipside. For instance, the comedian Paul Merton made an appearance. Michael deeply admired his talent and said that he had a very 'high regard' for him. However, as he also quipped, Merton had probably watched the original *Parkinson* shows in his pyjamas as a child.

Among the guests who turned up for the new run of *Parkinson* were pop singer Robbie Williams, actor Ewan McGregor, politician John Prescott (who played some drums on the show and regularly interupted Michael during his interview with Phil Collins, leading to the host pleading: "May I have my guest back, please?"), actors Liam Neeson, Helen Mirren and Joanna Lumley, and nature broadcaster David Attenborough. When McGregor and Williams were on, Michael surprised them by performing a tune on a French horn. It was a fantastic series that reminded anyone who needed to know that he was still the premier talk-show talent of British TV.

He received due praise from the critics. Even oft-bitchy television writer Victor Lewis-Smith was bowled over by his form. Wrote Lewis-Smith: 'There are no gimmicks with Parkinson, no casual sniping at his guests – just a respectful interviewer who's done his research and is proving, every Friday night, that the chat show wasn't dead after all. It was merely brain-dead. How refreshing it is to see an interviewer who doesn't regard every show as an opportunity to parade his own vast ego.' Lewis-Smith was fulsome in his praise for Michael's return, which he felt left other talk-show hosts in the shade. 'Where [Chris] Evans loves to scrawl graffiti all over his guests, Parkinson is more likely to ask for their autograph. Where Evans talks, Parkinson listens. And where Parkinson is as affable as a dolphin (albeit one that occasionally reveals a set of shark's teeth), Evans is more like a mackerel in moonlight. Shining, but stinking at the same time.' What a triumphant return it was proving to be: guests, viewers and critics were all delighted to see Michael back. For him, this was to prove to be a golden era, quite literally at times.

Fame, fortune, respect and a happy family: it seemed Michael Parkinson had it all. However, for a long time there was one glaring omission from his life. Considering the colossal influence he has had on the landscape of British journalism, both in the print and broadcasting spheres, it is of little surprise that he has accumulated hoards of awards and accolades. Such recognition is only to be expected and encouraged. What is more surprising, though, is that until 1998, Parkinson had only one award to his name. Speaking in that year, he said: 'Up until this year the only award I ever won was the *Sun*'s Performer of the Year back in 1972. That was all in 40-odd years.'

He had overlooked one particular award that he had won a few years later, however. It is understandable that he should want to forget that particular gong. '[It] was back in 1975, when my television chat show was in full swing and I was doing quite a bit of radio,' he recalled. 'I remember [that] I was on holiday in Portugal, sitting on a beach about a mile from the hotel. One of the porters came running down from the hotel and told me there was an urgent phone call from London. I raced back in the boiling heat thinking, my God, my parents have died. I grabbed the phone and it was a reporter who told me I'd just been voted the Best-Dressed Man on Radio. On *radio*! He asked for a quote, but I won't tell you what I told him.' He then remembers another award from the past: 'Oh, hang on a minute, I was once voted Best Haircut of the Year.'

At this point Michael was not showered with awards and prizes but all this was to alter in 1998 when the winds changed and he finally received a host of accolades. Suddenly, his mantelpiece was weighed down with honours and trophies from all manner of fields. Each and every one of them was, of course, entirely deserved and a fitting tribute to this talented, yet ever-modest man. 'This year I got nine awards for all kinds of strange things,' he said. 'One for Services to Comedy, one for Services to the Music Industry, [I was] made a Fellow of the British Film Institute, I got Yorkshireman of the Year, National TV Personality of the Year, Sony award for Radio, Best Sports Writer of the Year. And there's another one – oh, yes, Variety Club Personality of the Year.'

Starting with the Variety Club Personality of the Year award for 1998, Michael was characteristically humble when he received it. Described as 'modestly amazed' by onlookers, he told the star-studded audience at the Hilton Hotel in London: 'In a long, dull and uneventful life I have never had an award until today. When the Variety Club rang and said I was in the frame, I said, "I'm available."' The laughter and applause that greeted his appearance was testimony to the warmth and awe with which the public and professionals hold him. He has since donated royalties from his 1975 book *Parkinson* to the Variety Club. 'I decided to give the royalties to charity because I cannot claim the book to be all my own work,' he wrote. 'To The Variety Club of Great Britain goes the money, and it couldn't end up in better hands.' But what is this club?

One of our best-known children's charities, The Variety Club of Great Britain was founded in Pittsburgh, Pennsylvania on 10 October 1927, when a group of 11 men involved in showbusiness set up a social club which they named the 'Variety Club'. On Christmas Eve 1928, a small baby was left on the steps of a cinema with a note that read: 'Please take care of my baby. Her name is Catherine. I can no longer take care of her. I have eight others. My husband is out of work. She was born on Thanksgiving Day. I have always heard of the goodness of showbusiness people and pray to God that you will look after her. Signed, a heartbroken mother.' Efforts to trace the woman were unsucessful and so members of the Variety Club pledged to fund the child's living expenses and education. Later, they decided to raise funds for other disadvantaged children.

On winning the Yorkshireman of the Year honour (also in 1998), Michael was typically blunt and, well, Yorkshiresque in accepting it. 'For the first time in my life, I've started winning awards,' he said. 'You knock your guts off over 11 years and get ******-all and then you come back with one series of 10 shows and you win every sodding award there is, including Yorkshireman of the Year! I've been a journalist for 47 years; the only thing I've ever won was a vote for being second-best dressed man on British radio... There's a backhanded compliment!' Other winners of the Yorkshire gong include Alan Titchmarsh, Richard Whiteley and Britain's first black archbishop, John Sentamu.

Then came the award for services to music, given at the Music Industry Trust's dinner at London's plush Grosvenor Hotel. Past winners include Sir Elton John, Sir George Martin and Atlantic Records co-founder Ahmet Ertegün. Michael was surprised to join their ranks and expressed this in his trademark honest, self-deprecating and witty way. 'I've been lucky. I've had many awards in my life, but this is the most surprising one of them all,' he admitted, when told of the award. 'Blimey, for God's sake, I can't play a bar of music, I can't sing a note! I'm just delighted and baffled. As a kid, if I'd shown any talent for music I wouldn't have minded following it. I took my piano lessons. It lost the fight with football – it just couldn't compete.'

But David Munns, chairman of the award committee, said the decision to recognise the talk-show king was unanimous: 'Michael Parkinson is that rare person that has stayed at the top of the broadcasting tree for over three decades because what he says and plays on his shows has a resonance with successive generations of listeners and viewers. Parky's seal of approval has come to mean a great deal to many artists,' he beamed. 'His passion for music, enthusiasm for discovering and encouraging new artists and his ability to spot a winner is unique: every record label in the country would love to bottle his A&R talent.'

A BRIT School spokesperson joined in the tributes: 'Through his shows on television and BBC Radio 2, Michael Parkinson has became the UK's most important star-maker, being totally at the centre of success for a whole string of artists, who have gone on to sell thousands of albums – artists such as Katie Melua, a former student of the BRIT School, Michael Bublé, Jamie Cullum... all had their music brought to a mass audience, thanks to their performances on *Parkinson* and Michael's BBC Radio 2 show. His TV show is acknowledged by artists and managers to be the most influential in the UK for introducing new musical talent.'

BBC chairman Michael Grade, singer Katie Melua, songwriter and producer Guy Chambers and singers Chris Rea and Noddy Holder were among those who attended the Grosvenor event. It was hosted by Paul Gambaccini. Michael took the opportunity to reflect on the contemporary music scene. 'I was baffled to be chosen,' he said. 'I just put on the music I like – I certainly don't regard myself as a talent-spotter. But too many outlets just go for mass appeal these days. *The X Factor* is a good game, but it's got nowt to do with the kind of music I like. There ought to be an *Alternative X Factor* for all those musicians who can't get on television: creative people who don't just emulate others, but write their own songs. I'd be happy to judge it.'

Of course his pre-eminent brilliance in the field of radio was, sooner or later, bound to receive proper recognition. The only wonder was that it was so long coming. So, it was fitting that he featured in the 1998 Sony Radio Awards. Indeed, it was a fine year for the BBC in general. Out of 80 nominations, the corporation took 60. Of those, Radio 2 picked up 10 and Radio 1 received 9, compared with tallies of 7 and 9 respectively the previous year. Radio 2 was up for awards in 8 categories, including the Weekend Award for *Parkinson's Sunday Supplement*.

The first Sony Radio Awards ceremony took place in 1983, with just 35 commercial radio stations and 4 BBC Networks. Tim Blackmore, chairman of the Sony Radio Academy Awards committee said: 'The ongoing power of audio communication is more than amply demonstrated by the breadth and depth of these awards. Whatever platform was used to distribute their work, every one of our winners has demonstrated the kind of creativity, credibility or objectivity that has come to exemplify a quarter century of "the Sonys".' Among the early winners were Terry Wogan and Sue MacGregor, Radio Clyde's Richard Park and Radio City's Clive Tyldesley. Michael joined their ranks when he picked up the Weekend Award for *Parkinson's Sunday Supplement*.

By this time, his sports writing had wowed fans of football, cricket, golf and all manner of other games for many years, so when the *Press Gazette* named him their Sports Reporter of the Year for 1998, the selection was greeted with a mighty cheer from the journalistic touchline. Here too was recognition of Michael's unflinching ability to zoom in on the true charm of sport in his writing and then express it in a manner that was both eloqent and everyday. Consequently, he was also named *Cover* magazine's Best Sports Writer in 1999.

In the summer of 1999 he had to borrow a cap and gown

for a rather special ceremony at Hull City Hall. Michael was to be presented with an honorary doctorate by the University of Lincolnshire and Humberside in recognition of his contribution to radio and television. This was the same university where Mary had studied teacher training all those years ago: Endsleigh College on Inglemeire Lane. Michael was no stranger to the area either for he used to travel to Hull to watch cricket matches at the Circle on Anlaby Road. So it was a proud trip down memory lane for them both. 'Hull holds some very fond memories for my family,' he said.

Following the ceremony, a beaming Parkinson was quick to stress that he had not sought the award but that he was still proud and overjoyed to have been given it. 'I didn't ask for it, but I'm delighted to have got it and it has not cost any brass,' he smiled. He added: 'It is ironic really to be chosen to receive a doctorate when I consider that my time at Barnsley Grammar School were days I don't recall fondly. In fact, I hated school.' He was not the only celebrity to grace university honours award ceremonies during the late-1990s. Others included his dear friend and former Test cricket umpire Dickie Bird, who was honoured at Leeds University in 1997 and actress Helen Mirren, who collected a Doctorate of Letters at St Andrews in February 1999.

No doubt Michael heartily toasted his award from the University of Lincolnshire and Humberside and the same would have been true of the honour bestowed upon him the previous month. The All-Party Parliamentary Beer Group, formed as the Parliamentary Beer Club in 1993, exists to promote understanding among MPs of the domestic beer and pubs industries. Over 300 MPs and Peers of all parties are members. An officially registered all-party parliamentary group, the Group is the largest industry group at Westminster.

Each year the Group awards the title of 'Beer Drinker of the Year' to a public figure, who they feel has made a notable contribution to the world of UK beer or pubs, and in 1999 the gong went Michael's way. Other winners include Prince Charles, cricketer Darren Gough, Kenneth Clarke MP, chef Michael Roux and *The Archers'* character Joe Grundy. Michael is a popular figure among luminaries in the beer-drinking community. Mike Benner, chief executive of the Campaign For Real Ale (CAMRA) was asked who his dream licensee would be and he responded: 'Michael Parkinson. He is a good listener.' Cheers!

Cheers, indeed. It was at this time, as he received recognition across the board, from all corners of the world, that Michael took the time to reflect on where he was in his life and career. 'I was frightened about the show coming back – I was very concerned about it because times have changed and it was a long time since I had done a talk show. But it was interesting that we not only got back the audience we had before but we also got younger people watching, too.

'So there's obviously an audience which still likes talk. That's all it is. The show hasn't changed, it's just the same show as it ever was. I don't think you can change the format: a talk show is a talk show.' As ever, he remained unphased by his celebrity status: 'I didn't become famous until I was 35 so I wasn't dazzled by the fact that I was recognised in the street. The luckiest thing that has ever happened to me was being able to maintain a stable relationship. A good marriage is the spine of life.'

That same year, 1999, he was awarded a Fellow by the British Film Institute (BFI). The BFI promotes understanding and appreciation of Britain's rich film and television heritage and culture. Established in 1933, it runs a range of activities and services and has awarded more than 50 fellowships. The list includes such luminaries as Martin Scorsese, Dame Maggie Smith, Lynda La Plante, Gérard Depardieu and Clint Eastwood.

Such talk of recognition married to the customary acknowledgement of his wife showed just how content Parkinson was with his place in the national fabric. However, one of his proudest recognitions to date was yet to be bestowed. In November 2000 he was presented with a CBE by Prince Charles. The award was official recognition of his 'Services to Broadcasting'. On the day of the presentation Michael took his proud mother to Buckingham Palace with him to receive the CBE. Among the other guests to be similarly honoured was Lulu and he spoke admiringly of the legendary singer-songwriter: 'I remember Lulu from 1962 when she was a teenage pop star and she doesn't change. She's wonderful. In fact, she's even more beautiful now.' What a charmer! Lulu returned the compliment, saying: 'Parky is better than ever.'

Despite those kind words, the ever-humble Michael insisted he did not deserve his award: 'There are people receiving their honours here who have saved lives or taught somebody. What I do is fun... nothing more than walking down the stairs and talking to people.' Perhaps it was this sentiment that led to him almost forgetting to take his award home. He accidentally left it on a bench and only realised his error at the final moment!

As Prince Charles handed the CBE insignia to Michael, he inquired whether the presenter would wear it for his next chat show. 'I don't think I will,' was his modest reply. He added: 'I never thought about getting an award at all. What I do is fun. I never once woke up in the morning and thought, I've got to go to work.' Charles also enjoyed some banter with Lulu, who revealed: 'Charles told me, "You have found the key to eternal youth." That's a very charming thing for a man to say to a woman. The Prince even apologised that it had taken so long. It's a great honour and it was a real surprise.'

MP Paddy Ashdown was also there to receive an award and, like Michael, he was somewhat humble. Denying that he would wish to become known as 'Sir Patrick', he said: 'I've always been known as "Paddy" and will continue to be. It's very flattering. You feel very warm about it.' According to onlookers, Michael was one of the two guests who sent a surge of excitement through the crowd. 'Only Lulu and Michael Parkinson aroused the crowd to delighted applause,' recalls onlooker Nigel Nicholson. 'The rest of us, gathered for this ultimate accolade from our remote desks, laboratories and council chambers, looked modest in our hired tail-coats as we shuffled between the Yeomen of the Guard.'

Another award was soon on its way. Readers of *Reveille* magazine once voted Michael The Sexiest Man On TV. Michael said there were no feelings of jealousy in his household. Rather, his wife found it highly amusing: 'But it was never a problem in our marriage. Mary thought it was hilarious.' He was soon brought back to earth when he heard that a woman had written of him that he had, 'a face like a wrinkled testicle'. 'I was never vain about my looks – and still aren't, thank God,' he shrugged.

As well as receiving awards, Michael also presented some during this period. In 2000, he announced the results of the British Film Industry TV-100 poll. The winner of the Best British Television Show Of All Time was the iconic sitcom *Fawlty Towers*. This was a result that he approved of, as he explained when announcing the result: 'I'd have ordered a drugs' test if *Fawlty Towers* hadn't won.' It was a double triumph for *Fawlty Towers'* creator and star John Cleese as *Monty Python's Flying Circus* – the show that made his name – came in at No. 5. Five years later, *Coronation Street* was voted the Best ITV Show Of All Time. Michael again approved heartily, saying: 'I think life without *Coronation Street* would be unthinkable. It's part of all our lives.'

Just as *Coronation Street* is arguably one of television's biggest shows, so too was *Love Actually* (2003) one of the romantic comedy genre's greatest-ever movies. Directed by Richard Curtis, it included a host of cameo appearances by celebrities, including Michael Parkinson. The film features a character called Billy Mack, an ageing rocker played by Bill Nighy. He is aiming for the Christmas No. 1 as part of his comeback from heroin addiction. As he promotes his single – 'Xmas Is All Around' – on radio and TV shows, he knocks his own song, insults his manager and the boy band Blue and describes Britney Spears as 'the worst sex' he's ever had.

In one scene, Mack appears on *Parkinson*. During the interview, Michael says to him: 'This must be a very exciting moment for you, going for the Christmas No. 1. How is it looking?' Mack replies disconsolately, 'Very bad indeed. Blue are outselling me 5:1, but I am hoping for a late surge.' Mack then reveals that if he makes the Christmas No. 1 spot, he vows to perform on television completely naked. He asks Michael if he wants a 'sneak preview' and drops his trousers in front of him. Michael turns away from the scene and tells the camera: 'That'll never make No. 1!'

Among the other celebrities who appeared as cameos were Ant & Dec and DJ Jo Whiley. It was an effective move for the film-makers to make, as was noted by journalist Ryan Gilbey. Writing in the *Independent*, he ventured: 'Those actors will be balm for some viewers, as will the proliferation of cameos by TV celebrities such as Ant & Dec, Jo Whiley and Michael Parkinson, whose vocal acclaim the film has cleverly bought. Everybody wins – the audience is soothed by familiar performers, the celebrities are flattered that their popularity has been further ratified by this promotion to the cinema screen, and the film-makers can be certain that these double agents will use their media outlets to endorse the movie.'

Another newspaper, reviewing the film in a 'question and answer' style, wrote: 'AND WHO'S THE STAR? Who's *not* the star, more like. This is a real cracker of a Christmas tale with 22 leading characters getting fruity in festive London. Other big names include Colin Firth, Liam Neeson, Emma Thompson, Andrew Lincoln, Keira Knightley, Alan Rickman, Billy Bob Thornton, Rowan Atkinson, Michael Parkinson, Ant & Dec…' The review continued: 'PARKY? ANT & DEC? That's right. It's the Brit-flick of the year and everyone wants a piece of the action.'

In an interview Bill Nighy expanded on his role as rocker Mack and described how he worked with Parkinson. 'It's quite mad, but yes, we've produced the single to be released in real life,' said the 53-year-old actor. 'We're crossing our fingers and hoping that Blue are also going to release a Christmas single: I think we're going to wait and see what their release date is and bring ours out on exactly the same day.

'Don't put your house on me getting to No. 1. It would be funny, though. Can you see me strutting my stuff on *Top of the Pops*? But filming all that stuff was very enjoyable. Ant & Dec were completely charming. On the evening of that particular shoot, they were at least as concerned by how well Newcastle were doing in Europe as they were about their performance. People kept running up to them and saying "2-0". But they and Michael Parkinson were just great sports. I virtually exposed myself to Michael, but he took it all quite well under the circumstances and he was extremely keen and touchingly nervous about whether he got his lines right. It was a gas.' Michael's nerves reflect the excitement he felt at being included in *Love Actually*: 'It wasn't my big-screen debut – I made a film many years ago with Vincent Price. I can think of no greater honour I've had than to appear in Richard's film. I think it was an honour beyond parallel for me.' So honoured was he that he donated his fee for the appearance to the *Comic Relief* charity, which Curtis founded.

The film that he described as being from 'many years ago with Vincent Price' was *Madhouse*, made in 1974. Writing in the *All Movie Guide*, Cavett Binion said: 'This semi-serious horror film represented the first on-screen pairing of icons Vincent Price and Peter Cushing, who play, respectively, aging former horror star Paul Toombes and actor-turned-writer Herbert Flay, who unite in an effort to revive the popularity of Toombes' screen character "Dr. Death" for a TV series. Having recently recovered from a nervous breakdown, Toombes comes under suspicion when several members of the show's cast and crew are murdered in grisly reenactments of Dr. Death's greatest movie moments (as depicted in numerous colorful clips from some of Price's AIP films for Roger Corman). Though it at times aspires to the level of Price's classic of macabre humor, *Theater of Blood*, this film tends to stumble due to a middling script that dodges the opportunity to generate energy from the interaction of its two superb leads. Also known as *The Revenge of Dr. Death*.' A reviewer on the Internet Movie Database expanded on Michael's role: 'The part where Vincent Price is interviewed by Michael Parkinson adds some class to the movie and also some terror as the killer is stalking someone in the studio!' they wrote.

Michael was soon to appear as himself in another fictional

drama – this time the Australian soap *Neighbours*. The characters Karl and Susan visited London in a series of episodes of the popular soap that were broadcast in England in March 2007 and while they were over in England, they ran into a number of British stars who played cameo roles. These included former Spice Girl Emma Bunton and *Little Britain* stars Matt Lucas and David Walliams. The *Neighbours'* fansite *A Perfect Blend* outlined Michael's appearance: 'When Karl Kennedy and Susan Kinski were on holiday in London, they stopped to buy some postcards and as Susan went to pay, Karl was stunned to find himself standing next to chat-show host Michael Parkinson,' wrote the reviewer. 'Karl lavished praise on Parky, telling him what a great interviewer he was, before asking for his autograph. When Parky spotted the autograph of Pete Gartside in Karl's guidebook, he mentioned that he wouldn't mind interviewing him – or his Aussie mistress, and jokingly asked Karl if he could help him out, little realising that the mistress in question, Izzy Hoyland, had once been the other woman in Karl and Susan's relationship and was now carrying Karl's baby. As Parky bought his paper and walked off, telling Karl to give his regards to Dame Edna, Susan returned, disappointed to hear about the celebrity encounter she'd missed out on'.

Actress Jackie Woodburne who played Susan was honoured to have these stars included in the soap. She said: 'Michael Parkinson is a British icon. And Baby Spice, how cool is that? It was just spectacular. To go from filming in suburban Melbourne to London was great. I've been there several times before, but working there makes it more special because you're doing something you love.'

Just as *Neighbours'* cast members had flown to film in Britain, so too would Michael soon decamp to film a BBC programme. However, this would be a more serious show, one that resonated with his political history and drew attention to a worthy cause. Before then, he was to quiz some great names in front of an invited audience – only this time not on the *Parkinson* set.

One actor who proves that you can be a star and be grounded at the same time is actor and director Clint Eastwood. In 2003, ahead of the UK release of his film *Mystic River*, Eastwood gave an interview in front of an audience at the National Film Theatre. Michael was chosen to ask the questions. He began the evening in typical to-the-point style: 'The oldest adage in the business: the bigger the star, the shorter the introduction: Clint Eastwood. It's safe to assume you're among friends. We've just seen your film, *Mystic River*. I think it's bloody marvellous, but what's your feeling about it?' Eastwood replied: 'I haven't seen it yet.' No doubt relieved to be dealing with an artist less sensitive than Meg Ryan, of more later, Michael replied: 'That's a cop-out.' Eastwood was insistent, though: 'No, I've lived with it for so long – I've lived through the shooting of it, the editing and every other process along the way, so it's not for me to really judge at this point. I'll probably look at it again five years from now to get a fresh feel for it.'

As the evening progressed, Michael teased more and more interesting tales, insights and thoughts from Eastwood.

It was fascinating for the audience to see him perform live. The experience dispelled any doubts that the editing of the *Parkinson* shows was behind their smoothness for the presenter proved that he can keep the chat running smoothly with, or without, the benefit of editing.

He asked Eastwood about his view of modern-day moviemaking: 'I mean, you've just mentioned the special effects. Billy Wilder, a while ago, was asked, "What's a modern screenplay?" and Billy Wilder said, "The modern screenplay is where you build a set and then you blow it up." That would sum it up, basically, wouldn't it?' Eastwood replied, 'Yes, that would sum it up – nowadays you'd have many battles before you blow it up, but eventually you'd take it down. And that's okay, I don't heavily quarrel with that, but for me personally, having made films for years and directed for 33 years, it just seems to me that I long for people who want to see a story and see character development. Maybe we've dug it out and there's not really an audience for that, but that's not for me to really worry about.'

Michael ventured: 'I'm sure there is an audience, and I'm sure that audience has been neglected for a while as well in favour of a younger audience – it's happening across the board, in music, television and in movies as well.' Eastwood's response was: 'Yes, well there's the question: did the audience leave the movies or did the movies leave the audience? So, we keep trying.'

He then turned to more personal matters. It is interesting to note that he was far more probing than he had been with some other interviewees yet Eastwood did not seem to feel uncomfortable and was not at all surly. 'In an interview your mother gave in a documentary, she suggested that at this time you were travelling a lot up and down the country because your dad was looking for work and you were therefore fairly rootless, a loner, because you weren't any place too long,' said Michael. 'And she said that maybe that's where you started becoming an actor – it was the imaginary friends that you had to play with. Is that a wise observation by your mum?'

Eastwood paused for a while and said: 'Well, it's an observation. I wouldn't say that Mum was unwise, maybe so. I think kids are natural actors. You watch most kids; if they don't have a toy, they'll pick up a stick and make a toy out of it. Kids will daydream all the time. I daydreamed constantly. I was a mediocre student because I would sit in the classroom, the leaves would rustle and I would be off on a journey somewhere. So it was tough to concentrate in those years. But it's amazing, when kids concentrate on a game, to watch the intensity with which they do it. They can be extremely convincing.

'And the problem with becoming an actor as an adult is that as you grow up, you pile all these inhibitions upon yourself, and all the social mores. You get kidded by people as you're growing through your teenage years and into adulthood and then you're at the stage where you don't want to make a fool of yourself if at all possible. So, when I hit my 20s and wanted to be an actor, I had to think of how to strip all this stuff off and go back to when I was about 10 or 11 and I could just sit there and daydream and place myself anywhere and be anybody, anything that you were pretending to be and do it believably, where actually you would feel on the inside that this was you. That's all it takes and children are very good at this.'

Ever the fan of Western movies, Michael took the chance to ask Eastwood – who had appeared in so many films of that genre – whether he saw a future there: 'This is the 100th anniversary of the Western this year so I wonder if you'd be tempted by any offers to revive the genre?' Eastwood responded: 'You can't without the story – the story is everything. Whether it's a book or a screenplay, the story drives everything. And if you just go out and try to make one by putting on boots and jumping on a horse and riding off... If you don't have the material, the characters and the things to overcome and conflicts that give life to drama, you don't have it.'

Clearly there was an incredible rapport between the two men. This can partly be explained by the fact that although they were at the top of their professions, neither was keen on ostentatious displays of success or wealth. This, one might say, was true class. During their conversation, Michael picked up this theme: 'See, what's interesting about you is that you're this huge movie star and yet, if we read all the stuff that's been written about you, you've never been content and happy about that, even though a lot of people are. They just want to be the big star and they're happy with the limousines and all that stuff, but not you.' Eastwood took up Michael's point: 'I used to request that we don't ride in limousines. There's something to be said about being able to get a table down front sometimes but there's other times you just like to be the observer. You spend your life training to be an actor, observing people's characteristics so that you can design characters around what you've seen. But as a movie actor, once you've become known you're observed all the time so you don't get the chance to observe any more. You still get a taste of life but it's not quite the same and there's something to be said for a more anonymous life.'

The evening concluded with questions from the audience, with Michael chairing. It ended on a funny note. Michael's last question was: 'And finally, given your 50 years in the movies, if it all ended tomorrow, would it be a happy and complete career?' Eastwood mocked offence and said: 'He's got me on that perch again,' to general laughter. Michael said: 'I'm not trying to cut you off in your prime, I do assure you.' Eastwood quipped: 'I was feeling so good when I came in here, I'll go and have a check-up now.' Michael chuckled and wrapped the evening up: 'On behalf of everybody here tonight, thank you very much.' It had been one of his most enjoyable and memorable evenings.

Another star quizzed by him during this NFT season was Alan Whicker. Here, the pair had an easy way to relate to one another as Whicker too had been a chat-show host. Starting as a roving reporter on news magazine show *Tonight*, he moved on to present his own series, *Whicker's World*, and travelled the globe. Whicker has met and interviewed numerous stars, just as Michael has. This time, though, in front of a studio audience, he was the interviewee.

In introducing him, Michael made it clear what a special personal honour it was for him to share the stage, not least with a friend, but an inspiration too. 'Good evening, thanks for joining us on this special occasion,' he said. 'I'm delighted to be here tonight because not only is Alan Whicker a friend of mine, he's my hero. In the 1950s I saw a programme called *Tonight*. I was a young journalist working in Fleet Street and I thought if television has any kind of allure for me, it's this kind of programme. He set the standard, he set the style. Many have tried to emulate him, none have equalled him and nobody has surpassed him at all. Words are useless to go on and describe exactly what he's done. He's done more miles around the world than a second-hand Boeing, he's known to everyone in the business. He's revered by people like myself, journalists in the trade, as being the master interviewer and master TV journalist. Welcome, please, Mr Alan Whicker.'

Turning to Whicker's experiences in wartime, something Michael could relate to, given his own time serving at Suez and covering other conflicts as a journalist, the rapport between the two was clear. Michael said: 'Let's go back to the army days, briefly, because it's a dangerous job, in wartime particularly, and of course the equipment you were using in those days was primitive. I mean, there weren't such things as zoom lenses in those days, you had to put your camera on the front line, didn't you?'

Whicker replied: 'Absolutely. We did have some small telephoto lenses of no consequence but the stills men were using a Super Ikonta camera, which any Box Brownie enthusiast would spurn today, and our little DeVries camera was so ineffective. The Americans had Eyemos – we were very jealous of that. So they were shooting, these cameramen, without the benefit of being able to sit in a trench and see a close-up half a mile away. They had to be there. One of my sergeants in Sicily went into battle on the back of a tank. The rest of the crew were inside but he was on the back because he wanted to be there to get the pictures when things happened.'

Michael asked: 'But apart from teaching you the rudiments, the basics of filming that were to stand you in such good stead later on, did the war have a lasting effect on you? You saw battle, did it change your perspective?' Whicker paused and replied, 'I think not, to be honest. You never expect you're going to die, that's the first thing… You know you're invulnerable, and you know you're taking pictures, so you're not really a combatant. This persisted – I know it's quite ludicrous – but jumping ahead to the war in Korea, when I was a war correspondent, I simply assumed I was neutral. Nobody's going to kill me: I've got a notebook, and I've got a pencil…'

'I'm a hack, don't shoot me,' interjected Michael. 'Yes, it would be quite impossible for anything to happen because I'm just a spectator, really,' was Whicker's reply.

By now Michael was a grandparent three times over and naturally, this experience led him to consider his place in the world. Becoming a grandparent made him think back to his late father and he admitted to having strange dreams about him. In those dreams he would see his father at cricket matches, or see him with his grandchildren. They were evocative dreams that would stay with him into the following day.

He was close to all his grandchildren, describing himself as a 'hands-on, touchy-feely grandfather'. He added: 'I've got only one grandson, who I can play with and throw around. The girls are still a mystery to me, but I've got a very loving and tender relationship with them. They think, as they should, that their grandad's an easy touch, which I am completely and utterly. This summer we all went away together to Devon. It was a really beautiful family holiday.' He added, with a bit of a snarl, though: 'If we hadn't had to stop at motorway cafés on the way down and eat the crap they serve there for food, it would have been perfect.'

When his son Nick divorced his wife, Michael found this hard to accept and he also felt it had a knock-on effect on his relationship with the two grandchildren, James then 5 and Laura aged 8: 'They're lovely, but there's a sense of displacement in them which you don't get with the other grandchildren. Mostly their daddy is a long way away and it's not the same.'

Nick's divorce might have saddened his father, but it did not entirely surprise him. 'We had a hint,' he nodded. 'Nick was working in Australia, but we used to go out there every year. We could see the marriage fraying at the edges more and more. But there's not an awful lot you can do in that situation, is there? What you do learn is that if your children make a mistake in their marriage, you can't interfere. There are two people involved and you don't know the whole story. You've just got to let the relationship fracture and then pick up the pieces. We said to Nick: "Is it really over? Don't you love her any more at all?" He said, "No."

'So there was nothing we could do about it, but I don't understand – I can't conceive of a time when I would fall out of love with Mary.' As ever, his relationship with his wife remained strong. Meanwhile, he was winning prizes galore and was back where he belonged – presenting *Parkinson* on the BBC. What could possibly break up this happy state of affairs?

9

ON THE MOVE

With his feet back under the table at the BBC, and now that he was also a grandparent several times over, Michael might naturally have gone into 2002 feeling his life was reasonably settled. Once a man reaches his 60s, it is rare that he will have any spectacular upheavals in his professional life. Rather, this decade is normally the one in which he scales down work commitments and gently eases himself into retirement. But Parkinson's life has never been an ordinary one, so it should not be a surprise that his 60s turned out to be somewhat extraordinary. In fact, he had a huge professional upheaval in 2002, one that sent shockwaves throughout the television industry. Before then, however, he was to undertake his last major project for his current employers. It was to be an eventful, emotional and above all, memorable experience for him.

In the summer of 2002 Michael spent a week in South

Africa as part of a Sport Relief project, the biennial charity event from Comic Relief. He visited some of the poorest areas to see for himself how the work of the charity was targeted. Places he visited included a number of townships around Cape Town and Johannesburg, where people live in impoverished and also dangerous conditions. Among them was a secondary school in Cape Town, where sport was used to rehabilitate teenage gangsters, and a nursery in Johannesburg for very young children affected by AIDS. These were harrowing and emotional experiences for anyone, even someone as experienced and down-to-earth as the presenter.

The most headline-grabbing part of the trip, though, came when he fulfilled the dream of a lifetime and managed to meet and interview South African president Nelson Mandela. Michael beamed: 'I've always longed to meet Nelson Mandela. It was an incredible moment. Mandela has fought all his life for equality and justice, two values that are integral to the central core of what Sport Relief is all about.' His excitement was intense and almost boyish in its wonderment: 'Mandela represents all that is noble and proud in the human race – there is a lesson he can teach, *has* taught, all of us. One could say he is the nearest thing to a secular saint and if I have one ambition remaining in my work it is to interview Mandela, a man I have admired for many, many years.

'The interview will specifically be about him, his nation and the part sport has played in the downfall of apartheid,' he continued. 'Sport played a huge part in making clear the effects of apartheid. In the abstract, people may not have been able to bring to mind what it meant, but when it came to something as simple as black men not being able to play alongside white men, well, that was easy to understand. Mandela has a background in sport. He was a boxer in his younger days and he has written in his autobiography that during his imprisonment it kept him fit and that he would not have emerged the man he did without it. I think he was talking about more than the physical element, but about a mental and spiritual strength as well. I expect that is one of the things we will be discussing.'

Mandela was also delighted at the meeting, which gave him a chance to help the charity. He said: 'Sport is very important for building character because when you're involved in sport your individual character comes out: your determination, your ability to be part of the team and the acceptance of the collective effort is extremely important in developing your country as well as patriotism.' A Comic Relief spokesman explained the thinking behind the link-up. 'We thought it would be great to have Michael Parkinson involved, but who could he interview?' said Comic Relief chief executive Kevin Cahill. 'Well, Nelson Mandela has a passion for sport. He was a boxer and, as president, he led out the South African team when they won the Rugby Union World Cup. He supports the underlying aim of Sport Relief of helping young people, and it all fell into place.'

Michael's first observations of Mandela were physical, but ever the journalistic people-watcher, he quickly noted characteristics too. Later, he listed his first impressions. 'He is taller than I expected: straight, pencil-slim, elegant,' he wrote. 'He apologises that his dodgy knee won't allow him to walk down steps for a photographer.' He added that Mandela is clearly aware of the effect he has on people, but is careful not to abuse that power and is wonderfully good-natured. Not that the great man was scared to be a little cheeky when an appropriate chance arose, though. For instance, a cameraman was down on his hands and knees, searching for a plug socket, when Mandela appeared behind him. 'Is it not customary to say good morning to an old man?' he asked the stunned man. The President then observed that director Anna Gravelle was the only woman in the team and he told her: 'Remember, you must not let the men dominate you in your profession.' The meeting was barely minutes old, yet already Mandela had made them all laugh.

They met at 9am, by which time Mandela had already had two meetings. A tired PA of his told Michael that their day ends, 'When he has worn us out.' Then it was time for the interview. 'Mr Parkinson, I have to tell you before we begin that I am deaf,' said the President. 'I hope, sir, you will be able to hear my questions,' replied Michael. Mandela looked at him directly and smiled: 'I will hear the ones I want to answer.' Cue more laughter and a nice, light-hearted start to an interview that even a man as professional and experienced as Parkinson must surely have found daunting. Later, he admitted that he did indeed find the interview difficult, not least because it involved confronting Mandela about some harrowing scenes he had witnessed during his tour of South Africa.

And what scenes they had been. In his *Daily Telegraph* column, Michael wrote: 'My visit – the first I had made to South Africa – had a personal significance. More than 30 years ago, in the midst of anti-apartheid sports sanctions, I had been made aware that I would not be welcome in the country because of what I had written and broadcast.' Yet there he was, thanks in large part to the man he was about to interview. But first came his tour of the country. Initially they visited Cape Flats, where Michael was immensely moved by the plight of the people he met. He wrote powerfully of their situation in his newspaper column: 'We have been brought here by two 15-year-olds to see the kind of environment that is creating South Africa's appalling crime problem. There are 55 murders every day in this country and a rape every 30 seconds; in the Cape Flats, where we are filming, 30,000 young men are involved in crime. Without the prospect of work, and often missing a male role model in their lives, the gangs are their families. Prison is their school, ideal preparation for a future career.'

He then met some of those gangsters and was horrified by their attitude to murder and rape. He challenged them, asking if they believed it would be okay to refer to their mothers and sisters as 'bitches and whores'. They were shocked at this confrontation, but this was only the beginning of the courage demonstrated by Michael on this particular trip. He had to get the permission of a local gang chief merely to film in those areas. The gangster was 'a tense 28-year-old, who had spent 14 years in jail. He showed us his gun wrapped in a duster. He had a crown tattooed on his forehead between his eyes and four of his front teeth were missing.' Scary stuff.

The following day he passed the Saxon Hotel in Johannesburg's exclusive Sandhurst suburb, in whose luxury surroundings Mandela edited his diaries after his release from prison. Michael noted that within minutes of passing that location, they arrived in an area that he described as 'a hideous shantytown of bric-à-brac and tin. It looks like a gigantic scrap-metal dump.' Then came a meeting with people affected by AIDS and he painted a grim picture: 'We are here to film a team of women looking after victims of AIDS, not just the sick but also the children orphaned by the ghastly pandemic. Nearly 5 million South Africans are infected with HIV/AIDS – that is 10 per cent of the population. Every day, 1,500 more people are infected. In the hut where the women meet, an undertaker's list of coffin prices is pinned to the wall.'

Moved and angered by the situation, he noted that the tiny room used as a nursery for the sick children was rented. He decided to buy the property for them so that they would at least no longer be forced to pay rent. That evening they watched a local team play football and Michael, who had produced numerous sports reports in England in earlier years, wrote perhaps his most powerful account ever: 'The teams play in a haze of dust, which, added to the drifting smoke from the evening fires, filters the view across the township to the setting sun. Our bodyguard says: "There is an African saying: At this time of day, everything is beautiful."' Later that night he listened to a local talk radio station interviewing young South Africans from the townships. One was asked to describe himself: 'Broke, black and living in a shack,' he said.

The most shocking moment was yet to come. In his write-up of the meeting, he asked a rhetorical question of his readers: 'How do you interview a woman who has a few weeks to live?' The woman in question was Maria, a 26-year-old mother of two, who was dying of AIDS in a South African hospice. When Michael interviewed her, she lay, 'huddled under a blanket, curled into the foetal position, head against the concrete wall.' He found the interview too distressing to continue it for any notable length and, deeply emotional, he left the room. By the time he came to interview Mandela, he was full of despair at what he had witnessed. He asked the President whether he shared that emotion: 'I see an almost overwhelming problem. Don't you ever despair?'

They also discussed sport, as Michael later recounted. 'Sport has been crucial in bringing down apartheid. It has demonstrated the evil of apartheid to the rest of the world – when a black person couldn't play on the same team as a white one. Nelson is very aware of the power of sport as a political weapon. He told me that the boxing match between black American heavyweight Joe Louis and German Max Schmeling in the 1930s affected him. Hitler saw Schmeling as the ideal representative of the Aryan race, but Louis ended up breaking Schmeling's rib and winning the fight.' Mandela concluded: 'When you're involved in sport, your inner character comes out.' It was a sentiment with which Michael would have strongly agreed.

His trip rightly garnered him lots of praise. TV critic Simon Hinde wrote in the *Daily Express* that the interview with Mandela was a 'journalistic masterclass'. He added: '[In South Africa] his famed knack for getting on with people, for putting them at their ease, was employed to some greater purpose than helping a celeb plug a new film. He chatted to reformed and unreformed teenage killers and visited an AIDS orphanage in which a group of local women helped young children, many HIV-positive, to live something approaching a normal life. There was a particularly harrowing interview with an HIV-positive mother who had only days to live and had no idea what would happen to her two young children, who were playing happily outside.' The *Western Daily Press* ran the memorable headline, PARKY MEETS MANDELA AND BUYS A SCHOOL: THAT'S SHOWBIZ. Paul Hoggart, writing in *The Times*, said jokingly, 'We were witnesses to an historic meeting last night, between two elderly men. One, now internationally revered, returned in triumph to public life after a long period in the wilderness to spread his message of peace and goodwill to all. But that's enough about Michael Parkinson.'

But the final word must go to Michael himself. They say one shouldn't meet one's heroes, but he was only too delighted to have met his: 'Nelson is very tall, elegant and one of the few people I can think of who is universally admired. Sometimes I find people I interview can let me down by not living up to my expectations, but Nelson way exceeded any of my preconceived expectations.'

Despite having conducted this seminal interview for the

BBC, Michael was soon to move to pastures new. It might be football transfers that are more commonly discussed on street corners, beside water-coolers and in the pubs, but occasionally a television transfer also causes a huge stir. Michael's departure from the BBC was one such moment. In 2004 he created headlines aplenty when he chose to move to ITV. His announcement was kind, yet to the point. 'I'm very sorry to leave the BBC, of course I am,' he said. 'I have spent 20-odd years of my working life with the BBC and I don't turn my back on that lightly. But when the BBC brought back *Match of the Day*, effectively my spot had gone.'

He was asked how the BBC had responded to his decision. 'Of course they were not pleased,' he recounted. 'They were shocked in a sense because nobody saw this coming. But what can I do? Could I have stayed on doing a show I would be unhappy with? I think not, and I think they understood that.' Later, he discussed the end of his time at the BBC in terms not unlike those that one might use to outline the end of a romantic relationship. 'The BBC's reaction was bemused, like I was bemused,' he added. 'We just drifted apart. There was no big row and I'm glad about that because I've got nothing bad to say about the BBC. I'm a great supporter of the station and I'm sure what's happened won't affect our relationship. Of course I'm still working for them – I still do the Radio 2 show.'

After two decades, it is of little surprise that he spoke about his departure from the BBC in such an emotional way. It had by no means been an easy decision. He felt that when BBC bosses shifted his slot to accommodate the recently recommissioned *Match of the Day*, his natural place in the schedule disappeared. 'As soon as it happened, I said to the BBC, "There's a problem here, what are we going to do about it?"' he said. 'They said, "Oh we'll talk about it." Months went by and nothing happened, and I was within a week of being out of contract and they still hadn't decided.'

Surprised the matter had not already been cleared up, Michael returned to the BBC bosses. 'I went back to them and they said, "Oh Christ, we must think about that." They'd had months to think about it. They came back, suggesting they put it on a Wednesday night but I didn't want that, then Saturday night at nine o'clock.' But he disapproved of this time-slot. 'Too early,' he shrugged. 'Too easy to schedule against – it belongs at 10 o'clock.'

Asked to explain why the 10pm slot was so important, he showed his instinctive grasp of television and how it works. 'The thing about putting a talk show early is that it limits what you can get away with in a sense,' he said. 'It limits your guest options and the language on the show. Nine is after the watershed, but you get more of a problem. At 10 o'clock most things go. Not that the show is full of dirty talk but it can be a more adult show at 10 o'clock. And anyway, that's where it fits – that's where it always fitted.'

The media world is an especially gossipy one so it did not take long for ITV bosses to hear of the dispute. They moved quickly and offered Michael a 10pm slot on their channel. With the BBC still undecided, he snapped up the offer. 'It was as easy as that, and I sat there and thought, I've just left the BBC,' he laughed. 'And the BBC were going, "He's just left us."'

Despite being a wrench to leave the BBC, he remained certain that he had done the right thing: 'My view has always been that it's a talk show and talk shows belong after 10 o'clock,' he said. 'If it's at 9pm, it becomes something else, like a variety show. There's nothing wrong with that except I don't want to do it.' With his preferred place in the schedule gone, Michael took the sad decision to leave. 'If they haven't got the spot to give me, then what do I do?'

He remained entirely confident the show would be the same and that the channel would be the only thing to change. 'I'm a long way off retiring and I just had this predicament and it wasn't one I enjoyed sorting out. ITV gave me what I wanted, which is that 10 o'clock spot and the same number of shows I was doing for the BBC, and that makes me very happy. The guests won't change, the show won't change – all I've done is move the show over. It's a proven show and will work just as well on ITV as on the BBC.'

BBC1 controller Lorraine Heggessey was somewhat cool in her tribute to their outgoing star. 'Michael Parkinson is the doyen of talk-show hosts and it has been fantastic to have his show on BBC1,' she said. 'Parkinson's interview style was perfect for the viewer in the 1970s and 1980s when the celebrity world was still relatively naïve, but today's media-savvy stars just won't – and don't – reveal as much to him as their counterparts from earlier decades. So his defection should provide a real opportunity to take stock and breathe new life into an exhausted genre.' Would a simple channel and time-slot switch make any difference? 'We doubt it,' she said.

She concluded in more glowing terms, though. 'Despite the flagging format of the chat show, no one should belittle the wonderful legacy of unforgettable TV moments that Michael Parkinson has given us. He's one of life's great coaxers, is a born listener, and the fact that he's known instantly simply by that affectionate diminutive "Parky" places him firmly in that tiny elite of broadcasting's National Treasures, alongside such other greats as Wogan and Motty.'

All the same, her main sentiments seemed to be an attempt to appear unconcerned about his departure and in many quarters they received short shrift. Writing in the *Guardian*'s Media section, David Liddiment poured scorn: 'Don't be fooled by diary items suggesting that the BBC did not try too hard to keep Parkinson. The BBC was stung by the unexpected departure of one of its biggest stars and will now be telling anyone who will listen that Parky is over the hill. It did exactly the same when Des Lynam left the BBC following a similar highly secret raid. No sooner was he over the fence than whispers about Des being past it started to emanate from White City. Des and Parky do what they do with consummate ease. Talent this accomplished is hard to find and you lose it at your peril. As Bruce Forsyth [one of Michael's final guests at the BBC] will tell you, "over the hill" does not apply to this highly prized elite.'

As for ITV, they were delighted to acquire the signature of one of British television's most legendary names. Nigel Pickard, director of programmes, said: 'We're clearly over the moon. Michael is the very best and most loved in his genre. Television stars don't come much bigger than Michael

Parkinson. There's no doubt that he's the very best in his field and will be a fantastic addition to ITV's Saturday nights.' The media in general felt Pickard was rightly excited at the move. The *Independent* described ITV as having pulled off a 'Snatch of the Day'.

Mark Wells, the executive producer of *Parkinson*, explained how much work went on behind the scenes towards the end of the BBC era: 'We wanted to make it the gold standard of TV talk shows and were prepared to do whatever was required to maintain that position.' For example, the black leather chairs on the set were selected only after hours of discussion. 'They had to be made of the best-quality Italian leather, very contemporary, but with a nod to the past and the heritage of the show. Michael's last set at the BBC looked like someone had been to the office-supplies shop.'

Michael explained how three things made him feel assured on the set: preparation, preparation and preparation. 'In the end, it's about being settled yourself. It's about being at the top of the stairs and feeling, if I go on there now, knowing what I know, having prepared as I have prepared, sober and in my best suit, then if it goes wrong, it might not be my fault.' As such, he was always happy to reassure his guests. He once had to do this with Gene Wilder: 'I could see from that show [*The David Letterman Show*] he was nervous and doesn't like doing talk shows. He's jittery, so I had to reassure him that this wasn't like the Letterman show, all about jokes and standing on your head, being funny. On my show you can actually do an interview and talk. But I never say, "Look, this is what I'm going to ask you about." You can't rehearse an interview. If you do, the guest will turn to you, on-air, and say, "As I was telling you in the dressing room…"'

He remained pleased with his move, even though earlier on he had doubts about the transfer. 'When I first went to ITV, I thought, bloody hell, is this the end of the talk show as I know it? But I've enjoyed working to the new discipline – it's now a better show.' But the move must be seen in context. Benny Hill was one of the first high-profile channel defectors. *The Benny Hill Show* was on the BBC between 1955 and 1968. Hill was a massive hit and was awarded the 1965 BBC Personality of the Year award. Four years later, however, he moved to ITV where he remained for the duration of his television career. 'Going to ITV proved hugely successful for Hill,' said TV critic Garry Bushell. 'None more so because his programmes were sold to 100 countries. He developed his particular brand of humour there and most people now associate him with ITV.'

The following decade saw another surprising transfer. In 1978 the televisual world was rocked when Eric Morecambe and Ernie Wise defected to ITV from the BBC. *The Morecambe and Wise Show* had been a massive part of the BBC's output for the previous 10 years. Their 1977 Christmas special made it into the *Guinness Book Of Records* as having the largest audience of any British TV: between 27.5 and 28 million viewers, more than half the population at the time. When they were offered a financially lucrative deal, the pair moved to ITV, though. Their key scriptwriter Eddie Braben was contractually obliged to stay at the BBC and did not join Eric & Ernie at ITV until 1980.

At that time some people were hurt by the move. 'Forget footballers being bought by rival clubs or MI6 agents joining the KGB, the popular double act stirred up a tangible sense of national betrayal when they made space for commercials between their sketches,' wrote Anna Morrell in the *Western Mail*. 'We never quite forgave them and their demise was predictable.'

More recently, another high-profile Beeb man to make the pilgrimage to ITV was Des Lynam. Like Michael, Lynam was an institution at the BBC. He presented *Grandstand*, *Sportsnight* and *Match of the Day* and was the face of their coverage at top sporting events such as Wimbledon and The Grand National. However, in 1999 he defected to ITV, which had just acquired the rights to Premiership football. This turned out to be a mixed move, success-wise. The channel's coverage was unpopular among many fans and Lynam suffered as a consequence through no fault of his own. As TV critic Bushell said: 'It turned out to be a disastrous move for Lynam. The Premiership show was wrongly scheduled, going out early evening when most fans were still returning home from matches. No wonder ratings fell.' Not that it is always those who appear on the screen who defect. In November 2006 BBC chairman Michael Grade caused shockwaves when he too moved to ITV.

In the *Western Mail*, Anna Morrell added: 'Channel-hopping is a notoriously dangerous activity for key players in the world of television. It may be lucrative for those involved, but history shows it's an activity that greatly disturbs viewers. It's a phenomenon whose significance seems confined to the two key rivals in the industry – the BBC and ITV.' Not all commentators agree that the viewers particularly care about such changes. *Heat* magazine TV editor Boyd Hilton remarked: 'If Parkinson's just going to do the same show as he was doing on the BBC then I think the general consensus is a shrug of the shoulders.'

Certainly, the final edition of *Parkinson* on the BBC was nothing out of the ordinary. His guests included tennis ace Boris Becker, Irish pop group The Corrs and legendary entertainer Bruce Forsyth. Only the latter mentioned his impending move, saying that he should have brought an organ to play hymns on. He wished Michael luck with his move but the presenter himself was quick to push aside the issue's importance: 'It is not a solemn occasion, me leaving... No, no, it is only a talk show.'

This again underlines his professional nature. Many of today's chat-show hosts believe the entire show is all about them and their story. However, Parkinson was always keen to focus on the guests and wanted his last show to be business as usual. At the end of the programme, which also featured musician Jamie Cullum and comedian Patrick Kielty, he thanked his guests and as the studio audience broke into applause, he made no special comment or gesture, merely saying: 'And thank you for joining us. Goodnight.'

And thus ended the life of *Parkinson* at the BBC, where the man himself had of late been pulling in viewing figures of

Prince Charles presented Michael with a CBE in November 2000 for his services to broadcasting. Posing with Mary after the investiture, the crowd broke into applause.

Top: Throughout his career, Michael has always championed new music. *(Clockwise from top left)* Phil Collins, Cliff Richard, Elton John and Tom Jones are just some of the British stars to have performed on his shows.

On TV and his influential BBC Radio 2 show, Michael has often been the first to play debut songs by young stars such as Jamie Cullum *(left)* and Katie Melua *(right)*, a former student of the BRIT School *(above)* which has received the chat show king's support © *PA Photos/REX Features*

Michael counts as friends many of the thousands of people he has interviewed throughout his long career, including *(clockwise from top left)* Walter Matthau, Jack Lemmon, Spike Milligan, Joan Collins and Cilla Black. Others Michael describes as icons whom he has been honoured to meet, such as Nelson Mandela and Muhammad Ali *(inset)*.   © *REX Features*

Top: Michael is joined by Joanna Lumley to help BAFTA celebrate its diamond anniversary in December 2007. © *REX Features*

Bottom: On hosting duties again, presenting Dame Kiri Te Kanawa with a bouquet of flowers at the Classical BRIT Awards. © *PA Photos*

Top: The splendid Thameside house Michael and Mary share in the Berkshire town of Bray. The Royal Oak *(inset)* is the award-winning local pub owned by Michael and son Nick.

Bottom: Their garden is the perfect retreat from the London media frenzy, as well as a tranquil place to write and research.   © *REX Features*

Michael with the white Parky Rose at the 2007 Chelsea Flower Show,
which he dedicated to his father, a keen gardener. © *Rune Hellested/CORBIS*

A television legend and national treasure. Michael Parkinson with his Most Popular Talk Show Award at the National TV Awards.

up to 9 million. The new pastures of ITV beckoned and once there, his popularity was in no way diminished. As his son Mike Parkinson junior noted, if anything his father's popularity increased after the channel hop. 'Being his son, I suppose I have grown up with the show,' he said. 'I used to be in the studio as a child and watch recordings. What has taken me by surprise at ITV has been the reaction of the audience. When he walks down the stairs, it's quite extraordinary.'

Within these pages we've looked back at many of the triumphant interviews that Parkinson has carried out with celebrities, television moments to remember for all the right reasons – successful, memorable and often iconic. The Rod Hull and Emu episode perhaps stands out as an exception. However, there is one other interview that will be remembered, though not in quite so positive a manner: the one with actress Meg Ryan.

Born in 1961, Meg Ryan has been one of Hollywood's hottest names. During the 1990s she was the star of a string of successful romantic comedies, among them *Sleepless In Seattle*, *French Kiss*, *You've Got Mail* and *When Harry Met Sally*. In the latter, she performs a fake orgasm scene that has become one of modern cinema's best-known scenes. Back then, one critic titled her, 'the current soul of romantic comedy'. It had been quite a career for Ryan, who first starred on the screen in a television advertisement at the age of 18.

Lately she has attempted to reinvent herself as an actress and has played grittier roles in more serious films. It was one such film, *In The Cut*, which brought her to the studios of

Parkinson in 2003. Directed by Jane Campion, it is a psychological thriller in which Ryan plays the part of a New York professor of writing, who has an affair with a rough New York detective (Mark Ruffalo). At that time, Ryan had already earned herself a reputation as a difficult interviewee. She was perhaps in an especially icy mood because of some of the criticism the film had received. *Rolling Stone* described it as 'a mess', the *Los Angeles Times* said that it veered, 'between the baffling and numbing' while the *Guardian* called it 'perfunctory and unconvincing'. While promoting the movie, she had already shot down an interviewer. Referring to a question about her perceived image change, she snapped: 'This is not a conversation I am interested in because *you* do that. I do not cultivate image, you know, that is *your* job!' Even against this backdrop, it's hard to explain why she was so hostile during her appearance on *Parkinson*.

Up until then that particular show had been a fun affair. *EastEnders'* star Shane Richie revealed that he enjoyed dressing up as a child and was fascinated by actors wearing make-up at his local theatre. He then admitted that he himself wore red polish on his toenails: 'I think this is a throwback to when I was a child. People say, "Why do you do it?" and I say, "Because I can."' Two other guests that night were style gurus Trinny Woodall and Susannah Constantine. Woodall asked him: 'Do you wear women's underwear as well?' Richie replied: 'No, but I'll happily try them on, if you like.'

Laughter filled the air and the evening was going well. As

ever, Parky appeared to have pulled off a great programme. Then it was Meg Ryan's turn. Michael introduced her as, 'the beloved star of romantic comedies.' She then appeared and joined the stage. The first awkward moment came before she even sat down. She tried to sit on Michael's seat, rather than that of the guest. 'Don't sit in my seat, for God's sake,' he joked. He began the interview by adopting a segue from the previous exchange with Trinny and Susannah by asking Ryan if she found fashion empowering. Immediately she pulled a sarcastic face and replied, 'Do I find it empowering? Erm... not usually.' She continued, 'Did I just ruin your whole segment?' Michael reassured her that it was fine and pointed out that as a star, she faces a lot of media scrutiny over what she wears.

'Yeah,' she replied. He continued, 'What's your attitude to it?' But Ryan just shrugged, 'I just grin and bear it.' He asked if it bothered her. 'No,' she shrugged. 'I can see we're not going to get very far with this conversation,' he concluded. The audience laughed uneasily, as did presenter and interviewee. A swift moving on was needed and so Michael cleverly did just that, turning to her new movie. 'Tell me, tell us,' he stumbled, showing just how nervous he was, 'about the part you play.' Ryan then spoke at reasonable length, but with a reluctant air, about her character. The atmosphere somewhat more relaxed, Michael returned to a – comparatively – more difficult area. He pointed out that the director wanted to throw romance out of the window with *In The Cut* and asked Ryan why this was so. 'Why?' she repeated, and laughed condescendingly.

'Because she believes in love over romance.' Michael then asked if she believes there is a difference between love and romance. The pair then clashed over whether there is such a difference and if love is better than romance. Ryan insisted her view on the matter was 'beautiful', while Michael said it was 'promoting cynicism'.

Ryan then turned from interviewee into interviewer for a moment. 'Have you ever been romanced?' she asked. The King of Chat responded, 'Sure!' She asked whether it normally turned out well for him. He said it did and she pulled a dismissive, disbelieving face and asked, *'Really? Lucky, lucky you, dude!'* But he stuck to his guns and told her that she was saying that there is 'no happy ever after'. Ryan swept this aside and snapped, 'No, I'm saying exactly the opposite! That romance is something that is a delusion, whereas love, the reality of love, is more lasting.'

Realising they would have to agree to differ, Michael then turned to the part played by Mark Ruffalo. No sooner had he described the character as a 'foul-mouthed New York cop' than Ryan once again jumped in: 'That's so not how I think of it,' she said. 'And so don't think you're right.' Again, the audience laughed at the awkwardness of the situation. Keen to dispel the strange atmosphere, Michael touched her hand and said, 'We saw two different movies.' Again, the actress rejected his generous attempt to lighten the mood. 'Well, no,' she said quietly. Of Ruffalo's character, she said, 'He's a truth-teller, he's honest.'

As the interview crept along uneasily, Michael used the word 'woojie-boojie' as a polite synonym for sex. Ryan was sarcastic about the term. 'That'll get you a long way, that word, babe,' she drawled. He then turned to what he described as the 'graphic' sex scenes and wondered how long she needed to be with an actor before she could film such a scene. 'How long before he can kiss your bum?' he asked cheekily. 'The first day of shooting,' was Ryan's unconvincing reply. But he was having none of it: 'Come on, it wasn't the first day of shooting. This is a serious question.' In the end she admitted the sex scenes were shot on the last day. She then took issue with his description of the scenes as 'graphic' and insisted the viewer, 'doesn't see anything'. But Michael was incredulous. 'You don't see anything? You see the lot!' he laughed. Again, she was utterly uncompromising.

He then turned to a new area of questioning, pointing out that Ryan was once quoted as saying that acting was not in her nature. 'I *did*?' she asked. 'You did say that, yes. Are you denying you said that?' She conceded, 'It seems like something I'd say. I think what I meant was that it gets very awkward for me to be in front of an audience or in the spotlight; it doesn't come all that naturally.' He then asked a perfectly reasonable question, one that was surely on the lips of everyone watching: 'So, why do it?' Realising she was in a difficult position, Ryan simply replied, 'I don't know, maybe you could help me out with that?' Of course Michael is known to have always been a humane interviewer, willing to help out any interviewee who felt awkward, but such was Ryan's obnoxiousness that he wasn't about to let up: 'No, I couldn't! It's for you to debate and tell me. You can't have one [an acting career] without the other [fame], can you?'

The interview then took yet another turn for the worse, with the following uncomfortable exchange:

Ryan: You can certainly be an actor and not a movie star.
Michael: But you *are* a movie star.
Ryan: Yes.
Michael: By choice.
Ryan [sarcastically]: Seemingly!
Michael: So, you've got a problem?
Ryan: Yeah.
Michael: And seemingly not one that's going to be resolved on this show.
[Awkward silence]

At that point the audience's sympathy must have been placed entirely with Michael. Meg Ryan's behaviour, whatever the reasons for it, proved unkind and unnecessarily petulant. Michael had tried to conduct a friendly, professional interview and there she was, rebuffing his efforts. The viewers had watched countless celebrities sit opposite him and answer his questions so they were shocked to see someone behave so rudely.

He then changed the subject, asking Ryan about the fact that she trained as a journalist in her younger years. With this line of questioning, she perked up slightly and talked about her studies and how she changed career tracks to become an actor. 'What kind of journalist would you have made, do you think?' he asked. 'Nothing hardcore,' she replied, adding that she imagined she would have written for a magazine, perhaps about cooking.

There then followed this somewhat icy exchange:

Michael: Now that you're wary of journalists, does that give you an insight into what they're after?

Ryan [suspiciously]: Now that I'm *wary* of them?

Michael: Yes, you are wary of journalists. You're wary of me, you're wary of the interview. You don't like being interviewed. You can see it in the way you sit, the way you are.

Ryan: True.

Michael: Therefore, it's a perfectly easy question to ask you about being a journalist. In other words if you were me, what would you do now?

Ryan: Just wrap it up.

He then opened up the conversation to bring in his other guests, whereupon Ryan's body language was perceived to be dismissive of them. The returning the conversation to the two of them, he said: 'I'm going to go down another blind alley now. You were also quoted as saying that this was a film you probably couldn't have made three or four years ago.' 'No,' replied Ryan tersely. 'No, you couldn't have made it, or you didn't say that?' he struggled.

He then closed the interview by saying that he thought that Ryan had changed and had become a more wary and a more bruised person due to recent experiences in her life.

And he wondered aloud whether she might one day become a new Ryan, a happier Ryan. 'Maybe,' she shrugged. 'I hope to be there when it happens,' was his reply. The atmosphere remained awkward and frosty as the audience applauded.

This interview went down in the history books of awkward television moments. One is reminded of other chat-show interviews that went wrong, among them the infamous Bee Gees' appearance on the *Clive Anderson Show*. In the interview Anderson mocked the band's high-pitched singing style, their clothes and a former name of theirs. There were many memorably chilly exchanges, among them when Anderson asked: 'Were you working with Mickey Mouse at the time?' To which Barry Gibb replied: 'No, he got his voice from me.' Continuing to mock their high voices, Anderson said: 'Was it just the tight jeans?' He then told them: 'You're hit writers, aren't you? I think that's the word...' Robin Gibb replied, 'It's a nice word', to which Anderson replied, 'It's one letter short.'

But the interview took another turn for the worse when the Bee Gees revealed that they were once called Le Tossers. Anderson dived in with the inevitable punch line: 'You'll always be "Le Tossers" to me.' From that moment on, the atmosphere became frostier and frostier until the band walked out, with one member shouting: 'You're the tosser, pal!'

Another famous chat-show débâcle came in the shape of Grace Jones' interview on the *Russell Harty Show* in 1981. Jones slapped the presenter across the face after he turned his back on her to speak to the other guests on the programme. She said that she was being ignored. In 2003, television presenter Matthew Kelly used his appearance on the *Frank Skinner Show* to confront Skinner over his 'horrible' jokes about Kelly's arrest over a sex abuse allegation, of which he was later fully cleared.

In the aftermath of Parkinson's difficult interview with Meg Ryan, there was plenty of coverage of the episode. The *Sun* ran with the headline: MEG RYAN'S GRUMPY PERFORMANCE ON PARKINSON and the *Daily Mirror* chimed in, PARKY: MY MEG STRUGGLE. The *Evening Standard* even recognised the interview with a special award: 'The best car-crash TV award goes to Michael Parkinson for his interview with the completely uncooperative Meg Ryan.' Later, a poll of 2,000 television viewers resulted in this interview finishing third in a chart of most shocking television chat-show moments: 'The Hollywood actress, who was promoting her new film, *In The Cut*, became monosyllabic when answering Parkinson's questions. She ignored her fellow guests, fashion gurus Trinny Woodall and Susannah Constantine. The interview made global headlines.' UKTV Gold channel head James Newton added: 'These are the classic chat-show moments which people throughout the country talked about at the time and still remember with great fondness.'

Indeed, almost everyone who commented was sympathetic towards the King of Talk. But Ryan was unrepentant. 'I don't even know the man!' she snapped, when tackled on the topic. 'That guy was like some disapproving father! It's crazy. I don't know what he is to you guys, but he's a nut! I felt like he was berating me for being naked in the movie. He said something like, "You should go back to doing what you were doing." And I thought, are you like a disapproving dad right now? I'm not even related to you. Back off, Buddy! I was so offended by him.'

She added: 'I realised it's not like an American talk show where it's 7 minutes and then there's a commercial break. I had to do 20 minutes straight with this guy and I could either walk off – which wouldn't be good – or try to disagree with him very respectfully.' Not that many viewers would agree that her behaviour was particularly respectful.

Michael was more conciliatory. 'I should have closed it, but listen, it happens,' he shrugged. 'She was an unhappy woman, I felt sorry for her. What I couldn't forgive her for was that she was rude to the other guests. From the beginning Meg Ryan appeared totally disinterested – she's been through quite a change, mainly her divorce. I don't think she understood what was going on.' He could afford to be more upbeat: 'I afforded her the kind of interest and courtesy that she failed to demonstrate, either to her fellow guests or the audience. Having said that, I much enjoyed the interview and look forward to the next bout.'

Later, he admitted, 'She was just rude. She came on after Trinny and Susannah, who were talking about power-dressing, so I asked her what she thought and she said, "Oh, did you do a piece about fashion?" Of course she knew, she'd been watching it backstage before she came on. I thought, you cow! I mean, what can you do with someone like that? When she said I should "wrap it up," I should have said, "You're absolutely right, thank you and good night." I wish I'd stopped it right there, but I didn't – I went fishing for more horror.'

The manifestation of the support for Michael, not to mention contempt for Meg Ryan was clear in the press coverage. 'I felt it was very sad to see such an extraordinary display of arrogance,' said Mark Borkowski, a leading public relations consultant whose clients include Warner Brothers and Pavarotti. 'She is starting to show her age and is undergoing a bit of a reinvention, but she's going to have to work a lot harder than this. There's an American attitude that the mere fact they send stars over here means we should all genuflect, but in Europe people are starting to be more discerning.' Mark Frith, then editor of leading celebrity gossip magazine *Heat*, was of a similar opinion. 'Celebrities think that they can dictate the rules of every interview,' said Frith. 'Stars tend to clam up if they feel a question oversteps the mark, but Ryan should have been more communicative.' Members of the studio audience were approached for their own view of the evening, and again there was little support for Ryan. 'It was embarrassing to watch,' said one person. 'One of my friends was a real fan of Meg Ryan when we arrived – by the time we left he thought she was a prat.'

Judy Finnegan, who along with husband Richard Madeley has interviewed countless stars in her time, was also firmly in the pro-Michael camp. 'My heart went out to Michael Parkinson last week when Meg Ryan was so sullen and uncooperative on his show,' she wrote in her newspaper column. 'It's a hazard of hosting a talk show but pretty rare, as most of the stars are really nice – it's their entourages who are difficult. Our worst example of a sulky celeb was Andie MacDowell, whom we interviewed on *This Morning*. She was rude, difficult and sighed a lot. It gives me great satisfaction that now you hardly ever see her starring in films. Because she's not worth it.'

Eamonn Holmes is another experienced television interviewer who has quizzed star after star on the comfy sofas of *GMTV*. Again, his sympathy went out to Michael. 'I cringed when I saw Meg Ryan on *Parky*,' he said. 'She was the worst interview I've ever done. It was 1995 and I'd gone to Paris to meet her because she'd just finished filming *When A Man Loves A Woman* with Andy Garcia, in which she played an alcoholic. We knew her as a bubbly blonde in films such as *When Harry Met Sally* and *Sleepless In Seattle*. So I said to her, "Are we going to see a new Meg Ryan in this?" She looked at me and said, "Why, what was wrong with the old one?" Well, it was all downhill from there and the interview was a disaster. She hardly said another word to me.'

He then revealed that he felt so sorry for Michael that he even went as far as personally contacting him to offer his support. 'Parky is such a pro, he kept trying to get something out of her,' he said. 'I sent him a note after that just saying how much I sympathised with him because Meg Ryan is the worst person to try and talk to. I genuinely think she has a serious inferiority complex and if she wasn't being forced by the studios to do the publicity, she wouldn't speak to anyone.'

From the world of television interviewers and celebrity commentators, Michael certainly had plenty of backing. However, a more surprising voice of support came from Hollywood actress Gwyneth Paltrow, who described the interview as 'a car accident'. She added: 'I've never been so uncomfortable watching something in my life. I wish someone had explained to her who Michael Parkinson was before she went on. I think she was very defensive and didn't realise he was, like, this national treasure and everyone loves him,' she told London listings magazine *Time Out*. 'It was terrible. Then I thought, Oh God, I've got to go on this show.'

The final word on the matter goes to one of Ryan's fellow guests that night. Shane Richie later admitted that as the interview became more and more tense, he was tempted to try and lighten the mood. One of his plans was to turn to Ryan and say to her, 'Were you thinking of me when you did the orgasm scene in *When Harry Met Sally*?' 'But I didn't have the bottle.' Probably for the best, Shane!

Later on, during a television interview on an Australian show called *Enough Rope* that cast Michael as the interviewee, he looked back on the episode. 'There was a total lack of sympathy between the two of us,' he shrugged. 'I mean, she'd objected to a line of questioning I had about a film she made called *In The Cut*, which I didn't much like, and she obviously did – she was in it. And she took against me. She thought I was being kind of brutal and rude and nasty, and I wasn't, and she became defensive and awkward, and there's a marvellous moment where you know, when you can taste it in the audience, you can taste the embarrassment, you can feel... You owe it to them because it's good, you know.

'You're hemmed in by it, you know, and the guests are sitting there, paralysed and white knuckled like that, and I sort of was thinking of another way of getting out of this and so I said to her, "You've not always been an actress, have you?" "No." I said, "You wanted to be a journalist, didn't you?" "Yeah." I said, "What sort of journalist did you want to be?" "I want to be a journalist and ask questions to interviewers like you're doing." I said, "Well, if you were a journalist now and doing this interview what would you do?" She said, "Wrap it up." Such warmth! Reaching out to me, she was.'

Just as he was forced to contend with sensitive souls such as Meg Ryan on screen, so too has Michael sometimes had to tend to sensitive egos off screen. Former *Daily Mirror* editor Piers Morgan has found increased fame and fortune by publishing his diaries. In one series of entries, he recounts how he got the wrong end of the stick when he tried to arrange a lunch with Michael. Michael's sense of down-to-earth calm is apparent as he gently makes Morgan aware that a major snub he is imagining has merely been imagined.

'Michael Parkinson has invited me for lunch in a few weeks' time,' wrote Morgan in his diaries. 'Since I was sacked [from the *Daily Mirror*] I have more time to enjoy fun encounters like these, where I can turn my phone off, drink too much fine wine over amusing conversation, and then enjoy a long, lazy siesta afterwards. I eagerly accepted.'

In a subsequent entry, Morgan recounts how a new book about his old nemesis Cherie Blair has just been published by a journalist called Paul Scott. It includes an anecdote where, '...Cherie goes up to Michael Parkinson and starts laying into me, informing him that I told her and Tony that I wanted his chat-show job. According to Scott, Parky concurs wholeheartedly with her uncomplimentary views, and says I'll get the show over his "dead body".' Morgan then writes of his fury at the news, mentioning that Tony Blair once suggested to him the idea of taking over from Parkinson. Morgan reads into all this a 'typical piece of duplicity' from Cherie Blair, who he believes is, 'trying to turn Parky against me'. It transpires Michael cancelled their lunch date earlier that year and Morgan believed Cherie was responsible for the cancellation. 'This is obviously the real reason he cancelled our lunch date earlier this year. I sat down and fired off a hurt and wounded missive, saying Cherie's claims were all b****cks and that I sincerely hoped he didn't really think I'd behave in such a manner.'

Oh dear! Thankfully Michael was big – and witty – enough to see the funny side and to gently tease and reassure Morgan with his reply, which read: 'Dear Piers, you are not getting sensitive in your old age, are you? A cancelled lunch might have – and certainly did have – a perfectly logical explanation and nothing to do with "general frostiness" as you put it. I am beginning to worry for you, my friend. You need to buy me a large lunch and I will bring you a meaty shoulder to cry on. I will settle for a good bottle of Puligny-Montrachet and a signed copy of your disreputable diaries.

Shall we set a place for Cherie? Much love, Mike.' Morgan admits that after reading through the note twice, he laughed out loud at the realisation of his 'shudderingly embarrassing overreaction and pitiful whining'.

One of the most renowned interviews from the ITV reign of *Parkinson* was with Sir Bob Geldof. This time, the chat was memorable for the right reasons. The pair hit it off gloriously and Michael turned to Geldof's childhood, and asked him: 'Did you ever, in that period of school and after the loss of your mum, I also read something extraordinary somewhere that after the loss of your mum you actually used to walk round on your hands and knees?' Geldof replied: 'I forgot about that, my sister reminded me. For some reason I took to walking around like this...' [He then mimed walking with his hands trailing on the floor behind him, to great laughter.] Michael was laughing too, and asked his guest: 'You went everywhere like that?'

Geldof replied, 'Yeah, I'd get on a bus and go upstairs like it. And after a while, my father used to just put up with it. We'd be walking along the street and I'd be walking along like that – I mean, he is an extraordinary man. And that went on for about a year. But I did forget about that until my sister reminded me. But I don't know why, and I don't know why I did it. Yes, of course now I know. Anything to get attention, of course... Why else would you possibly do it? Unless you want to come back as a crab in a later life.'

From his angry punk records through to the legendary Live Aid concert, powerful political messages had been long linked with pop music for Geldof. Later in the interview the pair debated whether music actually changed anything. Michael asked him: 'This sense that you had from the beginning, though – politics and music. I mean, music in the strict sense has not changed anything, has it? It changes the way people feel, the way people move, but it doesn't change much politically. But what you've done, you proved that you can use your fame and celebrity to bring together a change that did change things. And that was Live Aid.'

There then ensued the following interesting exchange, which revealed much of both men's view of the world.

Geldof: Well, Live Aid did that, but I don't agree with you – I think that music does change things.
Michael: You think so – you think a song changes a politician's mind?
Geldof: Yeah, I do.
Michael: What examples would you give me?
Geldof: A couple of Bob Dylan songs. I think that music articulates a change that's happening in society before a society knows it's happening within them. So when you have The Beatles, for example.
Michael: But that's more reinforcement, isn't it?
Geldof: It is, but without being tossy about it – you know, what an artist does – and I'm excluding myself from this, but they tap into that which is happening anyway and articulate it back to society, and if that becomes a hit, it becomes a very powerful political tool because a million people perhaps are buying that one song and that can be used. And so when people are

marching in the streets and singing "Blowin' in the Wind" or "The Times They Are A-Changin'"' or something like that.

Michael agreed, calling those songs 'the theme tune to a revolution.'

It was intriguing to hear both men's views on the relationship between music and politics. Furthermore, it showed Michael was not a soft touch. At that point, Geldof was a national hero but his commendable work with famine and poverty was not enough to stop Michael from making his own views plain and challenging him on the question of whether music truly can change anything.

Another entertaining exchange was with actress Julie Walters in 2006. As he introduced her, he announced: 'No one plays mad and batty better than her.' During the interview, Michael asked her if she feared growing old. 'No!' was her reply. 'I don't fear growing old. I was 55 this week, everybody. No need to sing "Happy Birthday". No, I'm proud of being 55 – it's bloody great to get to 55! I've never been bothered about people knowing how old I am.' Michael schmoozed: 'You're looking wonderful.' Walters winked: 'You can come again, Michael.' Quipped Michael: 'I know I can.' Saucy!

Perhaps the most interesting portion of the interview dealt with Walters' relationship with her mother, however. Here, something came up which would go on to have much personal resonance for Michael. He said to Walters: 'It's amazing when you see the range of roles you play and what a wonderful actress you are, you really are. You had no training at all and you had opposition from your mum at home.' She nodded, 'Yeah, my mum didn't want me to go into it. When she heard she went mad, when I was giving up nursing, which was a respected – of course it is – and safe thing to go into. It's what she wanted to do nursing, that's why she wanted me to do it. And then for me to go – "You'll be in the gutter before you're 20!" I was, but it was rather nice!'

Asked if her mother was now reconciled to her choice of career, Walters agreed that she was. Michael asked how she discovered that her mother had accepted this. 'When my mum died in 1989 and we were dealing with all her stuff, I found in a little box all these cuttings that she'd kept,' she replied. 'She'd never talk about it, really. She would sometimes in front of other people. I'll never forget after *Educating Rita*, she suddenly realised people might know who I was. So, we were going along Bearwood Road where we lived and a friend of hers was coming the other way and I wondered what she was doing, she sort of veered me into this person so she could say, "It's just Julie, you know, she's just finished filming – *Educating Rita*, with Michael Caine." You know, as if he was some little extra. But there were all these cuttings, so you know.'

Michael replied: 'That must have been nice to find that, like a treasure trove of respect really, that she'd really been pleased all those years.' Walters responded, 'Yeah, and I think she'd have wanted me to find it.' Michael agreed: 'It's a lovely story, I like that.' It is eerie that he so enjoyed

173

this particular anecdote because, as we shall see, a similar event was to befall him when his own mother tragically passed away.

Beatle Sir Paul McCartney was another guest during this season. Here, Michael's memories may well have returned to his time at *Scene At 6.30*, all those decades earlier, when McCartney appeared with The Beatles and McCartney's mother asked Michael for his autograph. He asked Sir Paul: 'What you've never done in all the years you've been around, all the years I've known you, you've never become cynical, have you?' McCartney replied: 'I like it too much. People keep saying, "Why do you keep doing it?" I say, "Why shouldn't I? I love it." I'm not really that cynical type of person – I like what I do, you know, and as long as the audiences like it, this American tour has been fantastic, selling out, and so you know, why should I stop?'

Michael then turned to the question of advancing years, a theme McCartney had explored in some recent solo material. He asked him how much he felt he had changed as he got 'older and more mellow'. McCartney responded: 'When you're 18, you know, you don't wanna cry in case one of your mates catches you. I mean, my life was, I'd lost my mum a few years before that. John had lost his, but you wouldn't cry because you were 18-year-old Liverpool lads and you didn't do that kind of thing. I think now, you know, it's a good thing to do that and to open up to those emotions. That's the way I feel, anyway.'

John Lennon had been one of the earliest and most memorable guests on *Parkinson* in the 1971 series fatefully wiped from the archives, so Michael naturally turned to him there. 'When you're reminded and revisited by the memory of John, like we are now with the twenty-fifth anniversary of him being murdered, that would, I imagine, have a profound effect upon you?' McCartney said: 'Yeah, of course. I mean, it's so tragic, the circumstances in which he died, number one. You wouldn't even have to know him for it to have a profound effect on you. But if he's one of your best mates, that's very shocking. But you know what I find myself doing is remembering the great stuff, remembering the laughs and the hysterics. I get an image of the two of us walking around where we used to live, with our guitars slung on our backs before The Beatles, before anything had broken. With our drainpipe trousers, you know, well 'ard. You know, we didn't know anything was going to happen but we just felt great and you know, my mind goes back to all of that rather than the sad stuff.'

Perhaps the most newsworthy and controversial of all the interviews ever undertaken by Parkinson came with former Prime Minister Tony Blair in 2006 as he faced continued pressure over the Iraq War. He was also moving towards the final stages of his time in office and so there was interest in his relationship with his successor Gordon Brown. Naturally, the appearance was spun and hyped a great deal by both parties in the run-up to broadcasting. This guaranteed healthy viewing figures. Despite the fact that the interview caused an enormous political storm, much of it was light-hearted and not at all contentious. On the show Blair spoke of his most embarrassing prime ministerial moment at a press conference in France when he was asked if there were any French policies that he would like to imitate. Trying to answer in French, he replied: 'I desire your prime minister in many different positions.' Naturally, this provoked huge laughter on and off stage.

Michael then turned to marginally more tricky ground when he referred to the relationship between Blair and Gordon Brown, widely rumoured to be extremely frosty, when he ventured, 'The trouble is, Prime Minister, you keep saying, "Gordon and I are good pals," but no one believes you.' Blair smiled and replied, 'Yeah, but politics is very hard to have a friendship in... There is only one top job and it's not an ignoble ambition to want it, so there's all those difficulties there.' He brought the matter to a conclusion, saying: 'People have written that we are about to fall out drastically and go for each other for years and years and years, and whatever the difficulties, it's still a good partnership and one I'm very proud of. I'm proud to call him a friend and I always will be.'

However, the shadow of Iraq was looming at this time and much as the discussion of his relationship with Brown might have produced an awkward air in the studio, it was only when the conversation turned to the conflict that the atmosphere became truly electric. It is worth pausing at this point to consider the context of the interview. At the time, Blair was at the centre of one of the biggest political storms of all time and so he was unquestionably touchy about the subject of Iraq. Furthermore, he was also very sensitive about questions regarding his religion.

Tony Blair: That decision has to be taken and has to be lived with, and in the end there is a judgement that, well, I think if you have faith about these things then you realise that judgement is made by other people, and also by...

Michael cut in: Sorry, what do you mean by that?

Blair returned to his theme: I mean, by other people, by, if you believe in God, it's made by God as well and that judgement in the end has to be, you know, you do your... When you're faced with a decision like that, and some of those decisions have been very, very difficult, as I say, most of all because you know there are people's lives, not just, this isn't a matter of a policy here or a thing there but their lives, and in some cases, their death. The only way you can take a decision like that is to try to do the right thing according to your conscience and for the rest of it you leave it, as I say, to the judgement that history will make.

Michael was straight to the point: So you would pray to God when you make a decision like that?

Blair: Well, you know, I don't want to go into...

Parkinson: No, but, I mean, you've said that.

Blair: Yeah.

Parkinson: You've said that it would be informed...

Blair: Of course, you struggle with your own conscience about it because people's lives are affected, and it's one of these situations that I suppose very few people ever find themselves in, in doing, but in the end you do what you think is the right thing.

Naturally, the exchange caused quite a storm. The *Mirror* ran an angry article, in which fuming relatives of British soldiers fighting in Iraq vented their spleen. GOD WILL JUDGE THAT YOU WERE WRONG, MR BLAIR. OUTRAGE AT PM's IRAQ WAR 'ARROGANCE' ON PARKINSON read the headline. The *Daily Mail* ran with, UNDIGNIFIED, ILL-JUDGED AND SLIGHTY DERANGED, AS BLAIR TELLS PARKINSON THAT GOD WILL JUDGE HIM OVER IRAQ.

'Even Tony Blair's closest friends must be wondering whether he was wise to appear on ITV's *Parkinson* on Saturday evening,' read the accompanying *Daily Mail* article. 'He was, of course, guaranteed a pretty soft ride by the ever-emollient Michael Parkinson. An obviously handpicked audience had been primed to give him an ecstatic welcome.

'It was nonetheless a most undignified occasion. Whatever we think of Mr Blair, he is the prime minister of a great country, and to see him reduced to a diffident chat-show guest talking bashfully about his past and raking up unamusing old stories was deeply mortifying.'

The article criticised the prime minister for not appearing particularly embarrassed. 'This was the dumbed-down, touchy-feely Tony Blair, of whom it was impossible to believe that he ever had aspirations to be thought of as a great statesman. At one moment he even put his hand on the knee of his fellow guest, the American actor Kevin Spacey, who plainly hero-worships him.'

Those associated with the war queued up to have their say. Rose Gentle, a leading campaigner for Military Families Against The War, whose son Gordon was killed in Basra in 2004, aged 19, said: 'I hope my boy isn't with the same God

Tony Blair prays to. What kind of God would justify the deaths of thousands of people? If there is a God, He'll judge Mr Blair to have made the wrong decision – one for which I and many other British families have already been punished.' Colonel Tim Collins, who commanded the 1st Battalion Royal Irish Regiment in Iraq, said: 'As a Christian myself, I believe that, one day, we'll all be called to account by God for our actions. And if Mr Blair lied about why he was going to war, he'll have a big problem on Judgment Day. God doesn't start wars – men do. I'm sure God already knew there were no weapons of mass destruction in Iraq when Mr Blair was saying there were.

'He wouldn't approve of sending 103 soldiers to their deaths on a pack of lies and He wouldn't have planned a war without providing for the welfare of the Iraqi people. The fact that there wasn't any such plan – and hundreds of Iraqis are dying every day – suggests to me that God didn't have much to do with it.'

As for Reg Keys, father of Lance Corporal Tom Keys, who was killed by a mob in Majar Al-Kabir in June 2003: 'Forget God, I'll judge Mr Blair myself… and I find him guilty on all counts. He's guilty of not telling the truth, not showing restraint and not acting with integrity.' Keys, who stood against Mr Blair in his Sedgfield constituency in the General Election of 2003, added: 'God and religion has nothing to do with this war. Saddam wasn't threatening this country and don't tell me that Iraq is a better place. There are more people dying there daily than at any time before the war. Mr Blair is using God as a get-out for total strategic failure.'

While Blair faced a storm for his comments, not enough attention was paid to Michael's role in this episode. The man who at times is accused of being a fawning, gentle and bland interviewer was the same one who conducted one the most controversial television interviews of the early twenty-first century. There, he cut straight to the centre of a highly charged political issue, then threw in the ever controversial topic of religion, pressing the most powerful man in the country on those points. Hardly the behaviour of a soft interviewer, in fact it was quite the opposite.

There was a further hard-hitting and headline-grabbing interview on *Parkinson* when he quizzed Matthew Kelly. In a show broadcast in November 2005, Kelly appeared alongside football ace Thierry Henry and actress Sarah Lancashire. Michael quizzed him about allegations of sexual abuse (on all of which he was cleared) made against him two years previously. 'I have great difficulty talking about what happened to me in 2003 because it's very painful,' said Kelly. 'And also because it is three years ago and we kind of have to move on.' He was arrested while appearing as Captain Hook in a Birmingham pantomime production of *Peter Pan*. 'Based on an allegation made by an anonymous person of something you're supposed to have done 30 years ago, there is nothing you can do about it,' he told Parkinson, adding, 'what happened to me could happen to anybody, it's such an impossible situation. I hope that by what happened to me, people will learn.'

He acknowledged some of the tabloids had had 'a field day' with his arrest, claimed the desire of others to make money was at the root of the story, but said that he was still mystified: 'At exactly the same time, two million people were on the streets of Britain, baying our Prime Minister not to go to war with Iraq, and who was on the front page but some tart off some Saturday night TV show, who accused him of something that never happened 30 years ago. I don't understand that.' As Michael continued to draw him out, Kelly said, 'There was only one thing I really wanted to sue about and that was afterwards when somebody quoted me as saying, "My revenge will be sweet." I don't believe in revenge. I don't get it, I don't understand it. I don't see the point of it and I don't think the press should encourage that kind of behaviour.' Asked if he felt angry or even a victim, he replied, 'Do I look like a victim? You know, these things happen and we have to move on. You can be a victim, you can carry these things with you as baggage or you can embrace them and you can allow them to move you on. I would not recommend what happened to me to happen to anybody. I didn't want it to happen to me and I wish it hadn't happened to me. However, I wouldn't be without it now – because we are the sum total of the things that have happened to us.'

It had been a hard-hitting interview and the atmosphere in the studio was electric. Michael was both a probing and supportive host on a night that took on a far more serious air than a mere showbiz interview.

Not that he was about to leave showbiz behind on *Parkinson*. For whichever generation his guests came from, Michael always managed to show his professionalism by connecting with them. One such guest was Oasis guitarist Noel Gallagher, who appeared on the show in November 2006 to promote the band's compilation album *Stop The Clocks*. Gallagher explained some of the reasons why he had given up taking drugs. 'Nobody wants to look like a weirdo. [Pogues lead singer] Shane McGowan might want to look like a weirdo, I don't know,' said Gallagher, who had boasted of his previous heavy use of cocaine: 'My teeth were falling out and all sorts. You don't look good and everything revolved round getting hammered. I don't want it to sound like my drugs' hell... It was fantastic and I had some of the most monumental nights ever.'

Perhaps the moment that struck a chord most with Michael, however, during the interview was Gallagher's account of why he eschewed the rehab route when he gave up drugs. His quip that he didn't need rehab and anyone else taking that route should just give their money to him struck a chord with his own no-nonsense philosophy. 'It's just common sense really, isn't it?' agreed Michael. There was an air of Northern English bonding between the pair which transcended their different generations.

On Tuesday, 4 October 2005 Britain woke to the news that one of the nation's most loved and respected comedy talents had passed away. On a personal level, it was a day of immense grief for Michael. Ronnie Barker was one half of the double act completed by Ronnie Corbett. He was also an outstanding sitcom actor and scriptwriter, winning 4 BAFTA TV awards. Naturally, the tributes flooded in and Michael, deeply moved by his death, was at the forefront with particularly eloquent praise: 'Ronnie Barker had a wonderful career. He was one of our very greatest comedy actors. He wasn't a comedian, not by instinct at all. He was an actor with a writer's fastidious ear for a good script. He was a writer and was proud of his writing. He wrote very well indeed. If you look at his career, what's interesting about it was that he didn't do too much bad work. There was a very seamless series of very good parts through the years.' Michael identified *The Two Ronnies* as one of the great television partnerships in British entertainment history. He wrote of how Ronnie, a very shy man, was uneasy with the fame that came with the job, who preferred to observe others. 'He reminds me of Alec Guinness in that sense, that kind of shadowy figure who sort of circled around.'

On social occasions, Michael remembered that Barker was frequently inconspicuous. 'He didn't like such occasions but my word, when he took centre stage you had to watch him. He had that quality that you had to watch him. He was such a wonderful performer. The people who worked with him felt fortunate to work with him. He didn't have too many flops in his life, he chose well.'

Above all, Michael praised his professionalism. 'He was a wonderful actor to work with. You can see that in the work he did with Ronnie Corbett. They had a wonderful combination. He was a generous performer. Ronnie didn't try to be a star: he was a star. He didn't step centre stage and say: "I demand you look at me." You looked at him because he was very good at what he did.'

He then turned his attention to how Barker rated as an

183

interviewee prospect. 'He was impossible to interview,' smiled Michael. 'He didn't like it. I tried twice and we were friends for a long time. It was not because he was indifferent but he genuinely did not like talking about himself. He couldn't think why there was all that fuss. He was just doing a job to the best of his ability so he couldn't understand why people made such a fuss of him.'

As someone who had spent much of his career sharing and exploring the limelight with hundreds of famous interviewees, Michael saw Barker as 'an object lesson to a lot of people who seek the limelight with half his talent.' His longevity was down to talent, rather than gentleness; a talent to judge what worked and what didn't, drawing on years of experience writing.

Michael then revealed his favourite Barker character. 'My favourite was Fletch in *Porridge*,' he said. 'I thought it was a magnificent, rounded performance. It was a wonderful comic creation, yet a fully fleshed-out character. You laughed at him but there was also something about him that was much deeper and profound. That was Ronnie's talent, that was his genius.'

In 2007 journalist Ian Burrell spent a day and night behind the scenes at the ITV studios as an edition of *Parkinson* was prepared and broadcast. He described how, as Michael prepared to walk down the famous stairs for the 576th time in his career, he took a moment to compose himself on the little blue landing, lingering a while to feel properly prepared for the interviews ahead, in what had become an important little ritual vital for Michael to feel at ease and in control.

Earlier in the day there was a funny moment when Michael failed to recognise his guest Patrick Stewart. 'I saw Gene Wilder and there was a big well-made guy with a bald head and white T-shirt standing beside him,' he told Burrell. 'I thought, that's his bodyguard. So I started talking to Wilder and then realised that the bodyguard was Patrick Stewart! He did look different in this gym outfit. He's incredibly well toned, really fit – looks like my old army PT instructor.'

There had once been another awkward dressing-room moment when Michael witnessed David Niven being physically sick in the dressing-room prior to the show. However, Niven relaxed before his interview and once again it was all right on the night on *Parkinson*.

So the move from the BBC to ITV had not in any way diminished the quality of *Parkinson* as a show. Producer Mark Wells was full of praise for Michael, even to the end of the ITV period. He told Burrell that Michael: '…has a journalist's instinct, he's also a fan, in part, and he's genuinely interested in people. That combination makes him an extraordinary host.'

10

A SPORTING FUTURE

In 2007, Michael was on holiday in Australia with Mary. However, during his trip he also had some work to do, work he was very much looking forward to. The *Sydney Symphony* shows featured the Sydney Symphony playing a selection of music from movie classics, including *Gone with the Wind, Out of Africa, Breakfast At Tiffany's* and *Lawrence of Arabia*. Throughout the series, Michael shared his tales from over 35 years of interviewing the cinematic greats. 'There's some good tunes, you'll have a laugh,' he said, as he looked forward to the 2-hour 20-minute shows. 'And I'm going to sing. It's an old Yorkshire drinking song called, "Beer Is Best" – I've adapted some new Australian lyrics for it.'

One of Michael's best friends is John Barry, five-times Oscar-winning composer of scores for the Bond movies, *Midnight Cowboy* and more: 'So, all that comes together and explains my love for film music, and my involvement in the show this coming week,' he explained. 'The thing about a great film score is that you can set it to any action: it can make you sad or happy, whatever. You can play the picture against a great sound or great tune or make it work in support of the images. It's very interesting.' Michael is indeed more than interested in movie soundtracks: he's fascinated. He rates 'As Time Goes By' from *Casablanca* as his favourite movie tune. 'Has there ever been a more beautiful song than that? At least for my generation – there were more children born to that song than anything else!'

On the night, he was joined by charismatic conductor Brett Weymark, his orchestra and the Cantillation Chorus to recreate the magic of some of cinema's most famous scores: 'Moon River' from *Breakfast at Tiffany's*, the theme from *The Magnificent Seven* and the South American 'Getaway' from *Butch Cassidy and the Sundance Kid*. The shows were a great hit. The *Australian Daily Telegraph* reported: 'Music has always given film an emotional depth beyond the words being spoken or the action unfolding on the screen. Would the heartbreak of *Out of Africa*'s tragic love story provoke as many tears without John Barry's soaring, melancholy score? There were more than a few people attempting to dry their eyes as the Sydney Symphony performed the main title from that memorable film at the opening night of *Symphony at the Movies*, presented by the charming Michael Parkinson.'

One member of the audience painted a rather surreal portrait of the evening: 'Parkinson started with fart jokes (literally), continued with a Benny Hill style of humour that raised polite laughs, and by the interval had everyone whistling "Colonel Bogey,"' he said. 'For an encore, he sang some words he had made up to an ad jingle, which he obviously thought were delightfully risqué – something about horny and Warnie.'

However, in the midst of all the fun came the news that Michael's mother had been admitted to intensive care. For even the ultra-professional Michael, family must come first at such times so naturally he rushed back to England to be at her side. 'It is with much regret that I am unable to remain in Sydney for the final performance of *Symphony at the Movies*,' he said in a statement. 'I am very sorry to disappoint people booked for Tuesday night and hope they will understand this difficult situation.'

There was to be further and far more profound disappointment for his admirers when Michael announced that he was to make the following series of *Parkinson* his final one. The announcement when it came was short and modest, with no hint of the depth of the era he was bringing to an end. On 26 June 2007, he said: 'After three enjoyable and productive years at ITV, and after 25 years of doing my talk show, I have decided that this forthcoming series will be my last. I'm going to take next year off to write [...] and consider other television projects.' Typically, rather than indulging himself, he had time to offer gratitude to those who had worked on and watched his television output. 'My thanks go out to all those who have worked on the shows down the years and the viewers for their loyal support and occasional kind words.'

This was a major moment in the history of British

television. Viewers were saddened and dismayed to hear of Michael's forthcoming retirement. However, this was quickly replaced by a feeling of warmth and nostalgia as workplaces, pubs and street corners across the land witnessed scenes of people discussing the news and debating which had been the finest moments in the history of *Parkinson*. As for the man himself, he was later to add new insight into why he was hanging up his chat boots. 'Partly it's that I have been in this business for too bloody long and I'm beginning to get that Grumpy Old Man syndrome,' he said. 'It's a ridiculous posture, because of course things are different. When I started there were two television channels. Look at it now. Nobody knows where it's going, nobody knows what its future is, nobody knows in a sense even what its present is. It is a confusing world and I don't like being confused – I don't like that at all.'

Naturally, many journalists with their eyes on controversial headlines tried to lure him into being dismissive or even rude about his fellow chat-show hosts of the day, such as Jonathan Ross and Graham Norton. While characteristically honest in response to such lines of questioning, Michael was nonetheless unwilling to get into a slanging match. 'Theirs are comedy shows, not talk shows,' he shrugged. 'They are different animals. I am not trained to do it; it's not in my nature. I wouldn't last 30 seconds trying to do what Jonathan Ross does and he wouldn't last 30 seconds with a show like mine. I am not making a judgement either way; I am saying I don't think they will replace like with like – the entire landscape has changed.'

But he would miss the broadcasting outlet that throughout his multi-faceted career had been his favourite role. 'Of all that I do, including sports columns, television and a radio music programme, television is the most exciting,' he fondly beamed. 'From the moment you stand at the top of those stairs and hear that big band blowing you on, it's the most extraordinary feeling. It's a drug. You can't replicate that, standing in front of a big audience. You can't get any better than having your name on the billing. The rest is filling in. I shall miss it.'

And so came the time for him to put together the guest list for his final show. What line-up could possibly do justice to the closing of such a prestigious career? It was the moment for Michael to pick the chat-show equivalent of a fantasy football line-up. 'I was told to pick a wish-list and I put down these names and every single one of them is here,' he said of his dream team. 'They are friends who have made a particular contribution to the show. They are also people of great talent and interest and what a wonderful way to finish. The final show is a reminder of how lucky and privileged I have been to meet so many fascinatingly talented people. From Fred Astaire to Rudolf Nureyev, Ali to Ricky Hatton, George Best to Beckham, Jimmy Cagney to Tom Cruise, Ingrid Bergman to Cate Blanchett, Jack Benny to Connolly... I shall miss it.'

They say, 'It'll be all right on the night,' but for Michael, who had incredible back pain on the day the show was filmed, it nearly wasn't. He considered taking painkillers, but opted not to, for fear medication might cause his brain to 'get scrambled'. Instead, showing typical professionalism and courage, he chose to soldier on through the pain without any medical assistance. It proved a winning decision, as he revealed afterwards. 'As soon as [the show] started I'd forgotten about it,' he said of the back pain. 'It's incredible what the adrenaline will do. Then afterwards I got up to the Green Room and nearly fell over.' Once more, he had pulled it off. For each and every one of his *Parkinson* shows, he was a true professional and made a success of the evening.

On such a night it would be natural for even an old-fashioned Yorkshireman such as Parkinson to feel enormous emotion. He says, though, that it was only towards the end of the evening that he was hit by the true magnitude of it all. 'It's strange because it wasn't until afterwards that I suddenly realised what I'd done,' he said. 'I suddenly realised that, I stood in my dressing-room and I thought, I can't do that any more, I can't walk down those stairs any more, I can't hear that band any more, I can't get that wonderful feeling any more... When you're doing it, it's a mechanical process, it has to be. You have to get through it and do it as a show, so you think about it like any other show and it's not until afterwards that that wave hits you and you think, oh God, was I right? But I think I was: I know I was, actually.'

But not before putting together a cracking final show during which an end-of-term atmosphere prevailed. Plenty of jokes were made about Michael's retirement. Among the guests was comedian Peter Kay, who had started his career as a warm-up act prior to *Parkinson* shows of old. Kay cut straight to the chase and asked Michael: 'It's your last show, have you got anything planned?' Michael replied: 'Nothing as yet,' and Kay revealed: 'Got you a job…' He then produced a lollipop man outfit. Michael joined in the amusement of the audience and had a good chuckle at the gag. Kay joked: 'It's a great job – 20 minutes in the morning, 20 minutes in the evening – lollipop for the local infants' school.'

Another of his guests on that final night was Sir Michael Caine, who asked him: 'You are out of work when we finish, will you sign on?' Caine also revealed that he dislikes his voice being impersonated: 'They've got me on birthday cards saying: "It's your birthday today… not very many people know that." On Satellite Navigation Systems it's got me saying, "Take the second right and you will end up right in the s**t." People ask me, "Have you been doing Sat Navs?" I say, "No, I don't do Sat Navs or birthday cards." All they have to do is print, "This is an impersonation" and you can't do anything.'

His next guest was England football legend David Beckham, who was on good form. Beckham revealed some nice domestic detail about life at his home and also touched on his obsessive attention to detail. 'In our house in Spain we used to have this big rug that when you hoovered it, you could do it in lines like Wembley. Victoria used to catch me after the kids had gone to bed, doing the hoovering, and it would all be in perfect lines.' He added: 'I have to have everything in the right place and she finds it very annoying. Also cans of drinks in the fridge… I have to have four, four,

four instead of four, five, four. Odd things like that she has remarked upon.'

Inevitably talk turned to the day when Beckham relinquished captaincy, following England's exit from the 2006 World Cup tournament. This was a powerful, emotional moment: 'I remember waking up that morning, and I cried as I knew what I was going to have to do. I went into the press conference, cried all the way down to it, got through it and cried all the way back to the hotel. But I have had a great career on the England side.' So too had Beckham enjoyed a fantastic run down the years as a guest of Michael's. It is worth recounting here, in passing, how David Beckham played a part in one of Parkinson's most memorable moments. The second time he interviewed Beckham, the two men had adjoining dressing-rooms. 'The showers weren't working properly and he came round just in his pants and knocked on my door,' recalls Michael.

'He's got a great body – he's very lean. He's standing there looking like an archangel and says, "Can I use your shower?" He got out of my shower, put the towel around his waist and walked out to his dressing-room just as a secretary passed by, carrying an armful of files. She saw the most famous man in Britain standing in a towel and went "Oh!" and all the papers went flying! We helped her clear up and as she walked past me, she said, "And me, a married woman!" What a wonderful line!'

Back at the final show, his next guest was another famous David, this time another great hero of his: David Attenborough. The wildlife expert told a terrifyingly funny tale about an encounter with a rodent. 'The reason rats don't appeal to me is that the rat invades our living space. I was in India a while ago sitting on the loo and a rat appeared between my thighs.' (As one reviewer quipped: 'It's a mental picture of Attenborough I'll have difficulty forgetting for some time.')

One of Michael's favourite guests and best friends, Billy Connolly, also made an appearance. He began by joking that he was planning to write a Middle Eastern musical called *Saddam, You're Rocking the Boat*. This prompted a moment of emotion from Michael, who said wistfully: 'So much to do, and so little time.' Despite that note of seriousness, laughter is rarely far away when Billy Connolly is in town. The Scotsman referred to Michael's impending retirement when he said: 'Don't go! Don't go!' But this was merely a precursor for a punch line delivered in classic 'Big Yin' style. 'It's the only TV I get,' he complained. 'Nobody else will have me!' Michael saw the funny side.

There was also a musical interlude when Dame Judi Dench captured the mood of the evening when she sang a version of 'Thanks for the Memory' with re-worked lyrics that paid homage to Michael on his special night. 'It's time to say goodbye, I promise not to cry,' she sang. But she clearly seemed to have a lump in her throat and she was perhaps not the only one. Not that Michael would agree with widespread reports that he, too, shed a few tears at the end of the show. Indeed, he was uncharacteristically angry and foul-mouthed in response to the rumours. 'All this b******t about me being tearful, it was b******s,' he stormed. 'Anyone who was there knows it was wonderful. I didn't cry. Judi Dench cried because she was singing this very lovely song to me – but nobody else cried, for Christ's sake!'

It is likely that many viewers watching shed a tear for it was the end of an extraordinary era. *Parkinson* was first broadcast in 1971 on BBC1 and here was its final showing in 2007, this time on ITV. So much had changed during the intervening time. However, the constant had been that whenever *Parkinson* appeared on our screens, viewers were guaranteed an entertaining and insightful experience. Now it was coming to an end. No wonder such a wave of emotion swept the nation. Mark Wells, the show's executive producer, summed up this epochal moment. 'Truly, this is the end of an era,' he said. 'Michael Parkinson is one of the giants of broadcasting – his skills as a talk-show host are quite simply the best in the world. The *Parkinson* show has been a part of the British Saturday night for so long, it's hard to imagine life without it.' Paul Jackson, ITV's director of entertainment and comedy, added: 'He has defined the talk show in British television and no one has come near to equalling his record. His name is synonymous throughout the English speaking world as a benchmark for integrity and quality in the talk-show genre and being invited to appear on his show is a recognised landmark in any star's career.'

Despite many of these eulogies having something of the obituary about them, many broadcasting experts predicted that we had not seen the last of Parkinson asking questions on our screens. Elaine Penn of *TV Choice* magazine said, 'He is the sort of person who I think will be tempted back to do one-off interviews with topical people. I don't think it's the last we have seen of him.' She added that while Parkinson has been 'a legend in his own lunchtime' other broadcasters have been 'snapping at his heels' for a while, including Jonathan Ross: 'Jonathan Ross has taken the chat show and turned it on its head really, but Parkinson is definitely going out on a high.'

Jim White, the *Daily Telegraph*'s respected television critic, wrote of Michael's enduring appeal and what the viewing public would lose with his retirement. 'Parky has been there for a huge chunk of our lives,' he began. 'We haven't necessarily always watched his show but it has always been a comfort to know it was there in the schedules, however chaotic our changing world. The ticks, the mannerisms, the traits: so central has he become to our collective cultural vocabulary that you could have seen him for the first time on his final show and still immediately felt at home in his presence.'

Having correctly and eloquently spelled out the genius and appeal of Parkinson, he then continued with his tribute, by contrasting him with his heir apparent, Jonathan Ross. While in no way seeking to dismiss Ross's charm and talent, according to White, the contrast was clear for all to see. 'The point about Parkinson is that he knows how to ask a question,' he explained. 'It sounds a simple thing, but in his hands it is an art as refined as Oscar Peterson's piano-playing. Compare him to Jonathan Ross, his heir to the mainstream chat show. Largely because of his enormous salary, Ross has become something of a national hate figure.

This is unfair: he is a terrific broadcaster, an entertainer of panache and charm, a genuinely funny guy. What he can't do, however, is ask a question. Or rather, such has become the scale of his personality, his questions no longer have the power to elicit an answer.'

As for his old pal and regular guest Billy Connolly, well the Scot declared Michael would no doubt be back on our screens soon – and reckoned he knew why he'd return quickly, too! 'Once he realises there's no one to pick up the lunch tab, he'll be back,' he laughed. 'Tab pickingupage is a hugely important feature of showbiz because when you retire, you're on your own.' He added, 'that's what brought Frank Sinatra back. You realise no one's paying for the lunch or the fare any more. And when the phone stops ringing, that whole world dies.'

But the phone was soon ringing with some incredible news. On Saturday, 29 December 2007, just a fortnight after his final edition of *Parkinson*, Michael learned of an incredible honour. When he heard that he was being knighted for services to broadcasting, he was blown away. He was on holiday in Sydney when the news reached him. 'I never imagined it would happen,' he said. 'It's just fantastic, wonderful, a great honour. I haven't really taken it in. It's something I'll get used to, hopefully, in the coming years. What a way to end the year!' His wife Mary and his other relatives were also full of joy. Amusingly, one of his grandsons, Felix, asked if this meant he would be receiving a suit of armour. 'It takes some getting used to. It doesn't change you, but it makes you feel very proud,' he admitted.

Referring to his wife's new title, he said, 'I'm sleeping with a Lady now. It redefines our relationship.'

When Michael collected his knighthood at Buckingham Palace in June 2008, it wasn't the first time he'd been seen chatting to the Queen that summer: a few weeks earlier, Michael's personal assistant, Autumn Kelly, had married the Queen's grandson, Peter Philips. 'She asked me what I thought about the wedding and I told her I thought it was glorious,' said the newly knighted Sir Michael. 'We talked about that wonderful church, that chapel, St George's Chapel in Windsor, and I told her I enjoyed it, who wouldn't?'

In his usual down-to-earth style, he suggested his father would have not been quite so blown away by the news, had he still been alive. 'Well, he'd be baffled by it. I mean, he would still insist, I'm sure as he always did to his dying day, that I'd not had a successful life,' shrugged Michael. 'He was convinced I should play cricket for Yorkshire and just before he died, he said to me, "You've had a wonderful life," and I said, "Yeah." He used to come to all the shows. He said, "You've met some beautiful women." I said, "I have." And he said, "And you made a bob or two without breaking sweat." I said, "This is perfectly true, Father." He said, "But think on, it's not like playing for Yorkshire, is it?" And of course, he was right. And what he was defining was the difference between fame and immortality. If you play cricket for Yorkshire, you're immortal. It's like wearing the baggy green for Australia. You know, it doesn't matter: that's the accolade, that's the thing that you go for.'

As to the future, clearly we haven't heard the last of

Parkinson. 'Well, I mean, I'm not, people think I'm retired and I'm not going to work again, I mean, that's a nonsense,' he said. 'I've got 600 shows and 600 shows with some of the most extraordinary names in the twentieth and twenty-first centuries. So I mean, quite obviously there's something to be done there with all those 2,000 guests, there's some kind of way of repeating the shows or whatever, DVD compilations. I don't know, but that's what I will be working on as well and I've had one or two offers as well to do other stuff but I'll have to wait and see about that. I'm keen to watch a bit more cricket, actually and to get back and do a bit more writing, maybe a bit more journalism.'

Indeed, he soon returned to our small screens when he appeared in a television commercial for the AXA insurance group. A multi-media advertising campaign starring Michael was launched in early January 2008 and included both television and print advertising. The amusing TV commercial sees Sir Michael in a setting reminiscent of his *Parkinson* show, where he talks about how simple the group's Over 50 Plan is and explains the benefits. Mark Howes, managing director of AXA Direct, said, 'We are absolutely delighted to have signed up Sir Michael Parkinson to be the face of our new advertising campaign. He is known as a man of integrity and is instantly recognisable. As a straight-talking Yorkshireman, he is a perfect fit for a straightforward financial solution such as the Guaranteed Over 50 Plan.'

The next time Michael was back on our screens was on the Biography Channel in April 2008. Rolf Harris invited three accomplished artists to paint a portrait for Michael for the show *Star Portraits*.

He was also back in the public eye when he joined a campaign to keep the Windsor Fire Station (which serves central Windsor, West Windsor, Fifield, Winkfield, The Great Park, Old Windsor and South Datchet) open 24 hours a day. There were plans to make it a part-time fire station. Michael, who lives in nearby Bray, was not the first celebrity to back this campaign. 'Has any Fire Authority faced a more distinguished gathering of protesters?' asked Ephraim Hardcastle in the *Daily Mail*. 'The Queen, Prince Philip and Prince Andrew oppose Berkshire plans for ending 24-hour cover at Windsor. So do Sir Elton John, singer Natalie Imbruglia, Tony Benn and Wayne Sleep. Now local resident Sir Michael Parkinson has added his voice.' Michael was typically forthright in his statement: 'People who seek to close fire stations need their heads examined,' he snapped.

But this was not the only campaign he backed. In April 2008 he signed a petition against landmines and cluster bombs. The 'No More Landmines' petition was headed by Michael's friend Sir Paul McCartney, who said: 'Cluster bomblets, like anti-personnel mines, are unacceptable when they kill and injure innocent civilians, including children. I call upon individuals, organisations and politicians to do all they can to remove and reduce the impact of these weapons for future generations.' As well as Sir Paul and Michael Parkinson, other celebrities to sign the petition included Jo Brand, Jeremy Hardy, Emma Thompson, John McCarthy,

Davina McCall, David Walliams, Nelly Furtado, Boris Becker, Tony Robinson, Graham Norton and Rory Bremner.

There was a loud cheer in Michael's household when it was revealed in April 2008 that Craven District Council had pledged £15,000 towards the creation of a bronze statue of one of Yorkshire's biggest sporting icons, Fred Trueman. The council agreed to help fund the sculpture of the cricketer, which is expected to be sited at the top of Skipton High Street. Michael was particularly delighted at the news as he had been at the forefront of the campaign for a statue to be made of his cricketing hero.

He was overjoyed too when his pub, The Royal Oak, was recommended by *The Times*. The article said: 'Owned by Michael Parkinson and his son Nick, this village pub offers sturdy cooking that chimes well with the quality ingredients that make up the seasonal menu. Start with a beautifully executed Jerusalem artichoke soup with robustly flavoured anchovy toast, followed by a comforting combination of Cornish brill with brown shrimps, or roast grouse partnered with apple jelly, bread sauce, gravy and potato crisps fried in game fat.' The Royal Oak was also the venue for pre-wedding drinks the day Peter Philips married Michael's PA, Autumn Kelly, in nearby Windsor. Michael hosted the champagne party to mark Peter's final our as a 'free man.'

When mulling over offers to pen his autobiography, Michael was forced to contemplate how much things have moved on since his days as a journalist. 'I couldn't get on with the laptop because it didn't make a noise,' said the down-to-earth Yorkshireman. 'There wasn't that wonderful, empty sound of metal hitting cork, or the satisfying bang of the carriage return, which to a writer like me means progress. I couldn't possibly write 100,000 words of my life on anything but a typewriter, so when my little Fox portable exploded my son found an American company that provided typewriters from every period. I ordered the 1971 Remington – with 30 ribbons.' It was a similar model to the one with which he began his journalism career all those years previously. At first he was hesitant to write his life story. 'It indicated what I didn't want to do – to sum up, to finish. But as this is my last television series, it is a finish. It's been a funny life and I thought it would be rather nice to make myself laugh again.' A walloping publisher's advance must have helped to sway him too. He laughed: 'Let's be frank, no one in their right mind would sit down for six months writing a book for nothing.'

While television viewers may see a little less of Michael in the future, anyone who is keen to catch a glimpse of him could do worse than take up golf. 'I have already seen the perfect job for my retirement,' he quipped. 'It is at premises held by a middle-aged beach dweller in Queensland, Australia, who whiles away his days spraying suntan oil onto scantily clad young ladies – fun with ruin. Also, I have chosen his job, rather than similar occupations on beaches in other lands, because it is my experience that Australian beach beauties give you more to spray at.' He then added, 'With maturity comes the realisation that most ambitions are fantasies. I am never going to be a beach Adonis. Let someone else spray girls with oil on that beach in

Queensland. If I am going to spend my declining years standing in pools of sunlight then I haven't got the time for sitting in bus shelters, waiting for a fine day in Cleethorpes.

'Nowadays when the sun shines I am off in pursuit, golf bag on my shoulder, poacher-turned-gamekeeper, but totally unrepentant. The joy of golf is that even when the sun goes behind a cloud there is always a laugh to be had.'

One such occasion came when he was playing golf with Jimmy Tarbuck on a course in Surrey. Apparently, the English comedian harbours a fanaticism towards golf similar to the one Michael's father held for cricket. The course in question has a public footpath near to it. As Tarbuck was lining up a key shot, on which money had been staked, a passer-by interrupted to ask how to get to the nearby cemetery. 'Try dying,' replied the ever-sharp comedian, much to Michael's amusement.

Not that Michael's all-encompassing love affair with golf – he once said, 'If the greater part of this planet is water, at least two-thirds of what's left belongs to golfers' – is a lifelong affair, quite the contrary. Initially he began playing at his local club partnered by a man in his 70s. Michael tired of watching the man play with consummate ease while he himself continued to struggle. One day, in exasperation at another misplaced shot, he turned to his elderly partner and asked, 'Who on earth built this bloody golf course?' His partner replied, 'As a matter of fact, I did.' So it was that Michael formed the Anti-Golf Society. There, he shared experiences with other golf dissidents. One such story involved a man who was enduring such a lousy game that he threw his golf bag into a nearby lake in despair. Only then did he realise that he had left his car keys and some cash in one of the pockets of the golf bag. He slipped a disc while trying to retrieve it. His despair was complete when he returned to his hotel room and found his girlfriend in an amorous clinch with another man. Happy days!

Once attracted to the game's charms, Michael was soon head over heels in love. What he describes as his 'reluctant conversion' to golf began in Spain when he was playing with Jimmy Tarbuck, who was to become a regular playing partner. The pair loved to compete and, as we shall see, amusing incidents were rarely far away. At the start of the 1980s, his family 'moved into golf in a big way', he wrote. 'The wife, who took it up a year ago, now has more gear than Nancy Lopez. The children are practising hard in order to keep their father in some style in his later years and as for the head of the household, well, he is at that crucial point in the life of every golfer where you either throw the clubs away or succumb to a lifetime's addiction.' He took the second option and went about transforming his garden into a golfer's paradise. The shaded area of the garden, where their cat once happily kipped, was turned into a putting green. The cat did not take to this transformation happily and on occasion would use the hole as a toilet, making retrieval of the ball an unpleasant episode.

Michael has memorably recounted the differences between playing golf in Britain and Australia. 'Cleaning out the golf bag after returning from Australia was like looking at a scrapbook of our visit,' he wrote. 'I threw the sun block away, and the mosquito repellent. I also junked various sun hats and contemplated replacing them with a Balaclava. You think I jest. In fact, I am a great advocate of the Balaclava as an indispensable part of the wardrobe of a sporting gentleman.' He became fascinated, yet ultimately disenchanted, with the amount of coaching tips associated with golf, which began when he collected Mary from a golf lesson. 'Imagine my chagrin when I came across her with arms pinioned to her sides, trying to swing a golf club.' More disturbing was the fact that she was gripping a medicine ball between her knees. Where Michael comes from this would have warranted a visit from the vice squad. 'When I asked what was going on, I was told this was an exercise to enable the golfer to maintain the proposed posture at address.' As he drove his wife home, he says that he 'contemplated the kind of counselling given when a member of the family joins the Moonies.'

Michael then considered the raft of advice that he had been given down the years to improve his game and he wasn't sure that he liked what he found. He was once told not to grip the club too hard, to which end he was advised to imagine he had a dove in his hands. He was also advised to stand as if he were visiting the toilet, but also to imagine that he was perched on a pub stool and leaning over a fence. Another time he was told to imagine he had a bucket of water in his hands or to pretend that he was a windmill. Once he reached the peak of the backswing, he had been told that he should imagine his back leg was covered in plaster. And there was even more where that came from.

'So what we have so far,' he wrote, 'is a man sitting on a bar stool leaning over a fence while taking a leak, with his head stuck through a pane of glass and one leg in plaster. That's only the half of it and I still haven't hit the ball.' Ever the man of the people with his feet planted firmly on the ground, Michael advises golfers to put aside much of this instruction and instead simply concentrate on enjoying the sport. 'My proposition is that any human activity broken down into separate movements and analysed in such detail would become much more difficult than it ought to be, not to mention less pleasurable. Enough is enough... the next time you stand on the tee, I want you to free your brain of all the technical clutter, the mystical mumbo-jumbo. All you have to remember is the advice of the Scottish professional who said, "The right way to play golf is to go up and hit the bloody thing."' For the spirit of these principles he had many supporters, professionals among them. Michael praised Britain's number one female golfer Laura Davies' straightforward approach to the sport. 'She believes golf is fun and better than working in a supermarket,' he wrote admiringly.

Michael soon found it impossible to resist the lure of the pro-celebrity golf circuit and it is here that he can be seen regularly during his retirement. On this circuit, professional golfers rub shoulders and compete with celebrity golf enthusiasts, usually to raise funds for charity. His first game in this arena was a memorable one, which he described as 'a voyage into the unknown, like marriage or eating haggis, or entering a ferret-legging competition for the first time.' The invitation came in 1985. Looking back, he felt that he should have thrown it into a fire, but 'intoxicated by the flattery of the invitation, giddy with the innocence of one new to the game,' he accepted. It proved to be a memorable experience that he described as being 'as relaxing and jolly as the battle of Monte Cassino'.

With hundreds of spectators lapping up every moment, Michael's three playing partners all teed off impressively. However, his first shot proved a mere 6-in trickler. This moment of humiliation set the mood for the entire match. However, the final moment of ignominy came after the game. A young fan approached him with her autograph book. 'She asked politely for my signature and then busied herself finding an appropriate page. She flicked over the section marked "golf professionals" to which I could have no objection but also passed through the section marked "celebrities" which worried me slightly.' In the end she found what she was looking for: the appropriate section. She handed Michael the book. The page was headed 'miscellaneous'. 'Out of the mouths of babes and sucklings,' sighed Michael.

But he grew to enjoy better times on the pro-celebrity circuit, where he was awarded the nickname of 'Awesome Michael'. Soon he was competing with some famous golfers, including Nick Faldo, Gary Player, Lee Trevino, Ronan Rafferty, Tony Jacklin, Neil Coles, Howard Clark, Roger Davis and Ian Baker-Finch. This would have thrilled the ever-admiring Michael, who, despite his huge celebrity, has always continued to look up to his heroes. Here, as ever, he had found heroes to enthrall and inspire him and none more so than Nick Faldo, whom he describes as 'the archetypal working-class hero'. He admires Faldo for the fact that he has shown '…that by hard work and dedication you could take on the world and be the best. He is tall, fit and strong, with boyish good looks, size 11 feet and beautiful hands.' Although Faldo was aware that he was by then the best golfer in the world, according to Michael he remained 'no braggart'. He praises him for 'working harder than anyone he knows at getting things right. He leaves little to chance and genuinely cannot understand people who appear not to comprehend what he is striving for.'

He does wonder, though, why Faldo is not more loved in England, in the way that Frank Bruno and Gary Lineker once were. 'Is it that we are uncomfortable with true greatness? Are we perhaps misinformed by mischievous elements in the media who, for one reason or another, have it in for the likes of Nick Faldo?' Other golfing heroes of his include Bernard Gallagher, who reminded him of 'a physical training instructor I met in the army. This man made you feel scruffy just looking at him. Everything about him shone, from his burnished cap badge to his shiny black pumps. You could see your face in his pumps and I often did when he gave me 20 press-ups.' Gallagher was cut from the same cloth, he thought: one of those fortunate and blessed individuals who never looks crumpled. He also feels that Gallagher, who like him was born into a mining community, was 'an exemplary figurehead'.

Then came the day when Michael finally got to meet

female golfing heroine, Laura Davies. She was an hour late for the encounter at a Berkshire golf club but this did not dampen his enthusiasm one iota. An hour in her company was music to his ears. 'It is reassuring in the often loony world of professional sport, where half-formed youths are transformed into half-baked adults – and worse – to find someone like Laura Davies, who is both a genuine star and seemingly untrammelled by success.' He praised her 'frank and clear eyes... sustained by conversation which is straightforward and unpretentious' and was impressed by Davies' place in the 'sometimes neurotic and obsessive world of professional golf, where beta-blockers calm the palpitating heart, where God and Sigmund Freud are called upon to soothe the mental turmoil and coaches are witch doctors casting spells to ward off the yips.' In conclusion, he decided that the reason he liked her so much is because 'she can convey the will to win that all the great champions possess'.

There have been many happy days for Michael when his celebrity status and love of golf combine. One night in Australia he and some golfing chums celebrated Greg Norman's birthday at a poolside party. It was a raucous affair that culminated in Michael and the other revellers being thrown fully clothed into a swimming pool. While admitting he might have ticked his children off for such behaviour, he recalls that he 'couldn't wait' to tell them about the evening. 'Thus does hero worship make monkeys of us all, young or old,' he adds.

The following day he was out playing golf and his opponent's ball landed in a bunker. But his fellow golfer was not keen on moving his ball and so he asked why. 'Because it's landed on a scorpion.' Michael admits that after that he was very nervous of being attacked by a scorpion and for the rest of the day his game fell apart. However, on his return to England, he told the scorpion story and it was enough to scare Laura into losing the game that she was playing. It was two years since Michael had beaten her, so the scorpion cloud had a silver lining for him.

Another part of his sporting future comes with the Celebrity XI Charity Cricket Match that he organises each year at Bray & Maidenhead Cricket Club. Through the years such characters as Chris Tarrant, Rolf Harris, Rory Bremner, Kevin Whatley and Chris Evans have padded up to support the day. It's no wonder for the Bray & Maidenhead ground, situated on the banks of the Thames and overlooked by the Church of St Michael is widely acknowledged as one of the most picturesque in the country.

Naturally, the setting of Bray will be an ideal one for Michael and Mary's retirement. You can be sure that some of it will be spent in their local pub, The Waterside Inn, owned by celebrity chef Michel Roux. 'The Waterside Inn used to be a pub called The Riverside and I used to row down, have a few drinks and row back,' says Michael. 'The great beauty of that, of course, was that they couldn't arrest you for being drunk in charge of a rowing boat. Then Michel bought it in about 1972 and turned it from a pub into this extraordinary restaurant. We're extremely lucky because there are thousands of pub restaurants around, and only one Waterside.'

Roux is a friend and admirer of Michael's. He says he used to watch *Parkinson* a lot, but not so much for the celebrity guests as the chance to see the man himself in action. 'I learn a lot from the man, he is a pro,' he says. 'Everything seems to be so easy. He controls the situation and he lets people go their own way as well; I think he gets the best out of people. But on the television he is like he is in real life. He's not rude, he is not mean and that, I believe, is what true leadership should be about. When I look at my life, that's the way I am. You can still be among the best and behave well.'

Michael is equally kind about his special friend, Michel: 'He is very agreeable, very charming, and I don't think that's a front,' he smiles. 'I think he is that way, unlike his brother, who's much more pugnacious. They make a great double act: tough cop, soft cop routine. He's one of those men who, when you meet him, always smiles – he's never sullen or nasty. He always has this lovely twinkle and I would think that it's very difficult to confront him; he's beautifully balanced.

'He's a perfectionist. He's one of the very few who don't just talk about it, but actively pursue it. He's trained about 1,000 chefs here on scholarships. Most obsessives have faults, but he's certainly not as obsessive as most chefs are in the sense that although he's created this place, he's also done other things as well – there's lots more to him than just running a great restaurant. He makes me laugh. He's got a wonderful self-deprecating sense of humour, but also he's got this wonderful accent. Nobody can live as long as he has in this country and still have that accent.' Among the regular clients of The Waterside Inn are other celebrities, including Rolf Harris and Terry Wogan.

His future might be set to be a mixture of the sporting and the culinary but Michael can also count on having Mary by his side. As they move into their 70s, there is no sign of any fading of their love for each other. Michael believes they will stay together until death finally parts them: 'I just can't imagine divorce, I really can't,' he said. 'I can't contemplate life without Mary.' And what a life this extraordinary man has had. 'Listen, I've had a blessed life,' he smiles. 'When you come to the end of your life, that's the only really important thing. Nothing else matters.'

11

GOLDEN GUESTS

Over the years, Michael has had over 600 guests join him on *Parkinson*. All were memorable in their different ways. However, some inevitably stood out more than others. Many of these became regulars, returning several times to the show. Some even became personal friends of Michael. But all of them became, in their own way, golden guests...

Billy Connolly

Of all the guests associated with Michael, one of the most familiar faces must be that of Scottish comedy legend Billy Connolly. Indeed, the Scotsman credits his first-ever appearance on *Parkinson* as having changed his entire life. Born in 1942, William 'Billy' Connolly is one of Britain's all-time most successful comedians. However, it is possible we might never have heard of him in the first place, had it not been for Michael's initial and quite-by-chance championship.

John Fisher, the producer of *Parkinson* during the 1970s and 1980s, takes up the story of how Connolly came to be on the show for the first time in 1975. 'It was the first time we had booked an unknown,' he says. 'The show had been running for about four years by the time Billy came on. All our guests were big names – from stars like Fred Astaire to the [then] Poet Laureate, John Betjeman. Certainly, any comedy acts we had on were household names – Spike Milligan, Ken Dodd or Frankie Howerd. Here, we were giving an outing to a complete unknown.'

How had this come about? In early 1975, a somewhat hungover Michael was in a taxi in Glasgow, being driven to the airport. During the journey, the taxi driver asked if he had heard of Billy Connolly. When Michael admitted that he had not, the taxi driver pulled up and ducked into a record shop to buy a record. He returned to the cab with a copy of a live album recorded by Connolly, handed it to Michael and insisted he listen to it. 'Play that,' he demanded.

Michael had long since become used to being accosted by fans and relatives of artists keen to put the case for their associate to be on *Parkinson*. However, when he took the record home and listened to it, he was enormously amused by what he heard. Initially, he had not listened to the record on his return home, but his son Andrew encouraged him to do so. True, he couldn't understand everything Connolly said in his thick Scottish accent, but what he did hear had him in stitches. These included a sketch called 'The

216

Crucifixion 3,' which spoofs Christ's Last Supper as a drunken night out in Glasgow.

Michael told Fisher how amused he had been by this Scottish comedian, who was virtually unknown in England, and the producer decided to investigate further. 'I went up to a folk club in the north of England to see his act,' says Fisher. 'Billy was playing on the same circuit as Jasper Carrott and Mike Harding. What I saw, between the occasional song and banjo number, was a comedian who was entirely his own invention. I'm a great student of comedy and I've always claimed that if you show me a comedian, I can probably tell you who his influences are. But you do get ones who transmute into something that's totally their own. There are two comedians who are like that: Spike Milligan and Billy Connolly.' Fisher returned, utterly enthused by what he had seen of Connolly. He cornered Michael and told him: 'We've got to get him on.'

Connolly's first appearance on *Parkinson* came on 15 February 1975. Michael introduced him thus: 'First, someone who means everything in Scotland and as yet little down here. I say "as yet" because I believe this young man is one of the most original and best comedians I have heard in many a day. He has, in fact, recently appeared in a solo concert at the London Palladium, played to a packed house and triumphed. Nonetheless, his real fame remains north of the border. In Scotland, his two long-playing records have been the biggest sellers since The Beatles' *Sergeant Pepper* album. The man who made them has been called 'Scot of the Anarchic' – awful pun – and the Scottish equivalent of Lenny Bruce. Ladies and gentlemen, Billy Connolly.'

And thus appeared this extraordinary and funny-looking Scotsman, who was to become so famous around the world in the years to come. He started as he meant to go on: with the sort of risqué and surreal humour for which he has since become well-known. Always one to push the boundaries, he managed to get away with his risk-taking, thanks in no small part to his cheeky smile and that loveable glint in his eyes. 'I was completely ignorant of the ways of the world when I was wee, especially sex,' he told Michael. 'I used to ask guys in my class – you could only ask them so far – "How do you do it?" I think, in fact, for some mysterious reason I knew how to do it, although nobody had told me, but it was how you started that I wanted to know! From the dance hall to the house, and how do you get her from the living room into the bedroom, or do you just do it in the living room? I knew everything you did but I didn't know what order it came in. I remember there was a park near to where I lived, which was where I had my first experience of kissing. There was a line of seven of us and I was sitting and waiting for my turn with this girl, who was just sitting there waiting for us. When it came to my turn, I asked the guy in front of me if he could do it again as I hadn't got the hang of it.'

This sort of conversation would not be especially shocking in today's chat shows, but in the 1970s Connolly was definitely pushing the boundaries. He then continued to plough into saucier territory as he explained further his early education in the ways of the adult world. 'Later on in life, I used to read a friend's copy of *Forum* when I stayed there and he would give me a big pile of them when I was going to bed – on my own! It used to make me think I was awful dull. These guys going about in wet suits, firemen's helmets, whipping each other with leather rosaries... I thought I had better start taking my pyjamas off or something. There is no rule book, you see – nobody tells you if you are doing it okay.'

As Connolly went on to discuss, his relationship with women continued to be noteworthy once he became famous and performed live on stage. As ever, though, some hilarious imagery and punch lines were not far away. 'When I do a concert, it is always the women that laugh first and most. I think this is due to their position – in a sexual sense. I think they have a different attitude to sex and I'm glad they do, but they are very honest about sex. Whereas the guys are trying to be gentlemen and they are frightened to laugh before the wife does. I have played to a couple of audiences who haven't laughed at all, namely a crowd of drunk Scots in Brisbane. They even booed me on. They displayed all the tenderness of a dinosaur with its haemorrhoids on fire! "You're rubbish, Connolly, get off!" There was one guy that got up on stage and took my guitar off me and started swinging it above his head. He put my guitar out of tune and gave it back to me and then he starts chanting, "We want our money back" into the microphone and everybody joined in. I told him that he and I should go into the business together – we could be a pantomime horse: I would be the front, he could be himself.'

Michael and his audience were in raptures of laughter at Connolly's hilarious stories and his unique way of delivering them. It is more normal for stars to make their name before they come on a high-profile chat show. Here, though, was an up-and-coming act being launched on a high-profile chat show, all thanks to Michael's chance encounter with a Glaswegian taxi driver in 1975.

So what, asked Michael, was Connolly aiming for in his comedy? Who were his heroes? 'I set out to be a cross between Lennie Bruce and Robert the Bruce and arrived where I am, wherever that may be,' he said. With a twinkle in his eye, he added: 'My heavy thing is the body and its functions and malfunctions – the absurdity of the thing. Like farting, or "flatulence" as it is called and how people react to toilets. Like these ones where you all line up to have a pee and if you're really lucky, you get the VD notice right in front of you so you don't need to look at anyone – you can read that. You're frightened to look round in case somebody is smiling at you.'

Michael was well versed in the strains and pressures that pursuing a career in showbiz can foist upon people and he asked his Scottish guest what he did to unwind. 'I go fishing, that is my relaxation,' shrugged Connolly. 'I never catch any fish, but that doesn't matter. I love it and I think it's because when I'm fishing I think about fishing only, to the exclusion of absolutely everything. And most comedians are completely paranoid about their careers. For instance, when you read the notices, you can have nineteen beauties and one stinker. So when I'm fishing I think about nothing and my paranoia goes away.'

Pushing boundaries once again, Connolly cleverly and inoffensively then took on a major taboo topic. 'These are things that embarrass everybody, myself included, and you can chase the witch by talking about them,' he smiled. 'Another thing, racism is something I like talking about, but I very rarely do it because there are greater exponents of it than me. I heard a great racism-in-reverse joke: there were two black doctors in this hospital in Africa and they were walking along a corridor and one said to the other: "Did you tell that white guy in ward seven that he was going to die?" "Yes," the other one says. "You bastard! I wanted to tell him!"'

The two most memorable episodes of Connolly on *Parkinson* involved far more risqué humour, however. On one occasion, he made a joke about flatulence that famously had another of the night's guests – American film and television actress Angie Dickinson – in stitches. Connolly began the routine with a gag about his star sign. 'It's pyrex – I was a test-tube baby. I do know it does work: once I was on stage in Washington DC and a guy threw a pipe at me, a smoking pipe. And it hit me right there [points to his head]. And I fell and I felt really stupid, the shock of it coming through the spotlight and hitting me. And I got off-stage and I was shaking. It was the first night of an American tour and it wasn't my audience, it was Elton John's audience. They made me feel as welcome as a fart in a spacesuit.' There was laughter throughout the studio at this final gag. However, the image of Angie Dickinson's face as she truly grasped the meaning of the spacesuit line will linger long in the memory of all who saw it. It's a joke that has been replayed many times and is made all the funnier by Dickinson's embarrassed, almost reluctant, laughter.

However, the most standout moment in all of Connolly's appearances on *Parkinson* was his very first appearance. It was a shocking joke in many ways, but a combination of his charm and perhaps the era in which it was told meant that not only did he get away with it, he still managed to use the appearance as a springboard to gaining popularity in England. Right from the start, he warned that it was a controversial story. He began: 'A guy came up to me on the street – I hope I can get away with this, it's a beauty,' and looked at Michael with a cheeky smile. Returning to the joke, he recounted what the guy in the street had told him. 'He said: "Hey, Big'un!" You know, in Scotland they call me Big'un. I'm not very big but everyone there's awful wee, you know? But he said: "Did you hear about the guy who's done his wife in, and that?" and I said: "No." This guy was going out to meet his friend in the pub and he asked how his wife was. His friend said, "She's dead. I murdered her." The guy said, "You're kidding me? I'm not talking to you if you keep on talking like that." And his friend said, "Please yourself. I'll show you, if you want." So they went up to his tenement building, through the close – that's the entrance to the tenement – and to the back green and into the washhouse. And sure enough, there's a big mound of earth, with her bum sticking out. The guy says, "Is that her? Why did you leave her bum sticking out?" He said, "I need somewhere to park my bike!"'

From this controversial joke, Connolly launched a whole

career. Though some might find it distasteful, it was enough, in Billy's own words, to change his 'entire life'. Michael, in a subsequent documentary called *Billy Connolly: Erect for 30 Years*, revealed that people still remember Connolly telling the punch line to the 'bike joke' three decades after that TV appearance. Asked about the risky gag, Connolly said, 'Yes, it was incredibly edgy for its time. My manager, on the way over, warned me not to do it, but it was a great joke and the interview was going so well, I thought, oh fuck it! I don't know where I got the courage in those days, but Michael did put confidence in me.'

'I will never forget it,' says John Fisher. 'You always get nervous before the performance of each guest. You live it with them and you know, before they do, whether or not they've been successful. With Billy, you knew right away that he was a huge success. I will never forget that bicycle joke – sort of risqué, but completely harmless.'

Parky said at the time: 'Of all the people we have had on the show, we never had a bigger single reaction than when we had Billy on first time around. He's a huge star!' However, despite Connolly crediting *Parkinson* with launching his career, Fisher humbly shrugs off the accolade. 'I don't think any of us can lay claim to making his career,' he said. 'When there is talent like that, someone else is always going to come along and discover it. He was so different. He wasn't an Oxbridge-type, like Peter Cook or Dudley Moore and he wasn't part of the traditional comedy scene, like Les Dawson or Morecambe and Wise. Everyone has a "first appearance" to get through and everyone needs a little luck. And every now and again someone makes an appearance that sets the whole country talking. That's what Billy did.'

As well as their professional relationship, Michael and Connolly also enjoy a close personal one. 'We have a shared background and aspirations,' explains Michael, of the early impact the Scotsman had on him. 'It was like he was talking about my life. I saw him as a class warrior. There was a political edge to his humour, as if he was saying to working-class people, "Look at me, if I can do it, you can, too."'

Connolly appeared eight times as a guest on *Parkinson*. 'I'm not certain that he made more appearances than anyone else,' says John. 'People such as Kenneth Williams and Peter Ustinov were regulars on the show for two or three years before Billy appeared on the scene, but it was always an event when Billy was on. There were people at the Beeb who would say, "You're having him on *again*?" But Parky and I knew that if Billy did the show, it would probably be the only TV he did that year. He was so busy with other things. It almost became the Billy Connolly Show with Michael Parkinson.'

In 2002, Michael hosted *Billy Connolly – A BAFTA Tribute*. During the evening, he paid Connolly a tribute that resonated, professionally and personally, for the Scotsman. 'He has made me laugh more than any other human being,' said Michael.

Muhammad Ali

'I'm the greatest!' is just one of the self-aggrandising statements that Muhammad Ali was fond of making. Born

Cassius Clay in January 1942, he is a former three-times World Heavyweight Champion and winner of an Olympic Light-heavyweight gold. In 1999, Ali was crowned 'Sportsman of the Century' by the BBC. He was also legendary for his spoken words and as such was a superb guest on *Parkinson*. 'I did four interviews with Ali, one of which I did with him and Joe Frazier on the eve of their second fight at Madison Square Gardens,' smiles a nostalgic Michael. 'I couldn't imagine nowadays you wanting to put two boxers together to do an hour on a TV show, but Ali was a remarkable human being, as was Frazier in a very different way. To do that interview two nights before they fought was remarkable.'

The most explosive encounter, though, came in the standard *Parkinson* studio in England. Michael asked him why he sometimes fights people who are 'quite obviously' not in his class. An already-testy Ali replied: 'Like, for example, who?' Michael said, 'Well, let me put an even better question. Do you...' Ali then interjected: 'See him get out of that! Well, let me put it another way. Things are getting hot. You see him drinking that water?' Even putting such a controversial question to a boxer is surely proof that Michael is no softy. He then returned to the question by raising Joe Bugner as an example of the boxer referred to in his initial question. Again, Ali was enraged. 'I don't like the way you write about Bugner,' he snapped. He said that he thought it was a shame to put Bugner down, that the British lacked the ability to unify. 'Look, you've got a good White Hope there. You can build the man up, give him some confidence and might make him be better than he is. He's representing

England, you should stand up for him – he's your champ.' But Michael was not about to back down. He said that what Ali had said, 'Cuts no ice at all,' adding that he felt Bugner had 'no class'.

Ali was also not in the mood to back down, as befits a boxing champion, and he said that he thought Bugner had more class than George Foreman. He then took a cheeky turn in the conversation and suggested that maybe Michael was so critical of Bugner 'because he stole your girlfriend, or something'. For some time, they debated back and forth the boxer's merits. The debate continued, with Ali asking Michael if he could box. He replied that no, he had never boxed. Ali said: 'Well, why do you know so much about boxing? You got a good television show and a good script.' It was hardly the sort of exchange that a fluffy chat show would have hosted.

Ali then got even more personal with Michael, comparing him to other broadcasters. He said: 'Supposing I told you, supposing I told you you'd never be nothing and you're not as good as David Susskind, and you're not as good as Eamonn Andrews, or you can't make it like Harry Carpenter. Anyone tell you that? Now look at you, you're the number one man around here, but you had to work up.' The point of Ali's diatribe was to show that such criticism as Michael was giving to Bugner would only make the boxer train harder, for the chance to prove him wrong. 'I'll tell you one thing,' he concluded, 'people like you are good. I admire people like you because it makes you train, it makes you work to prove you wrong.'

It had been a feisty exchange. However, a far more explosive debate was to come when Michael turned to the movement that Ali was involved in, which preached separatism between black and white people. 'Now, isn't there a contrast there?' asked the host. 'You belong to a faith which teaches separatism, yet here you have white friends.' Ali snapped: 'You say I got white friends, I say they're associates!' Michael asked, 'You don't have a single white friend?' Ali admitted he did not and denied being friends with Angelo Dundee. 'He's an associate,' he insisted.

The discussion continued in this vein for some time, then Ali turned a question onto Michael. 'It's a fact that white people hate black people. Listen, listen, what do you mean it's not true?' Michael said that of course it was not true that white people hate black people. Ali called Michael 'the biggest hypocrite in the world' for saying this. Michael simply reaffirmed that he didn't dislike black people. 'Oh you don't, I know you all right,' said Ali. However, he added that 'white men talk about us and don't like us.' Michael told Ali that he was 'missing the point'. The boxer hit back that Michael did not, 'have enough wisdom to corner me on television. You're too small mentally to tackle me on anything that I represent.' He insisted he was serious, saying: 'You and this TV show is nothing to Muhammad Ali.' Ouch!

Later, Michael questioned Ali on what education he had missed out on at school. He asked the boxer whether he was illiterate when he left full-time education. 'I have a wisdom that can make me talk to you or an educated man on any subject and if the audience or the people listen, they'll say I won,' was his reply. He added that when it came to common sense, to feelings, love, compassion and 'heart for people' then he was not illiterate, but 'rich'. They were difficult areas that Michael was quizzing Ali on, and as a result he revealed sides to his character that were profound and would become legendary.

On a more straightforward, yet still entertaining note, he asked the champion if he could build a boxer who was able to defeat him, what qualities that boxer would need to have. Ali replied: 'He'd have to be about my height, a little taller. He'd have to be about one-tenth of a second faster. He'd have to hit real hard, he'd have to be faster than me on his feet; he'd have to be more experienced. And when you add it all up, it ain't nobody just going to come along like that. They've got to build themselves up and I'm going to see them when they're building. Nobody is going to start fighting tomorrow and have those qualities.' The interview concluded with Ali telling Michael that he had 'caught him' during the interview. Michael replied jokingly: 'You won't trap me, man, you won't trap me.'

George Best

Born in May 1946, George Best was arguably Britain's finest ever football talent. He won the European Cup with Manchester United in 1968. However, he won more than that: he also acquired the hearts of fans across the world with his nimble, tricky football genius. Best received numerous personal awards and across Northern Ireland the admiration for him is summed up by the local saying, 'Maradona good, Pelé better, George Best'. He also found fame for being one of the first celebrity footballers and for his alcoholism, which ultimately took his life in November 2005.

Best was a regular guest on *Parkinson* and became a close friend of Michael's. Some of the finest accounts of his remarkable fame and how he coped with it come from his many chats with Michael. For instance, on an early appearance he said: 'It was a bit weird. I mean, [his agent] was stuck in a little office in Huddersfield receiving 10,000 letters a week from girls sending their knickers. It aged him very quickly. Obviously there's a lot of protection, hopefully people have learned that you need good back-up. I have it today.'

During another early appearance, the football legend tackled the question of whether he was still in debt to the public in some sense and neatly kicked the idea into touch. 'A lot of people have asked me: "Don't you think you owe the public something?" I'm not sure whether I do or not. I think I've given – I like to think I've given something for 9 years anyway... But I couldn't take what was going on outside of that. You know, a British footballer will play between 55 and 70 games a year, sometimes 20 times a month, and at the end of it you do what you're told, really.'

By this stage, Best was giving exceptional insights into the life of a professional footballer. However, Michael teased out further detail from the Manchester United legend. Indeed, just as Best once danced around defenders, so too did Michael tease the best out of his interviewee in the studio.

'So, for 11 months of the year, you can't sort of go mad, you've got to be in bed at reasonable hours and you cut the lights completely,' said Best. 'And I think it was a whole lot of strain, I think so. I mean, when I was first in trouble, when I started talking about being under pressure and strain, at the same time there were, I think, three or four other First Division players who were having trouble. And I think if they'd have been single, as I was, and not married men with responsibilities, I think they would have done exactly the same as I did.'

With the interview flowing along nicely, what, wondered Michael, were the added complications of being the most famous footballer in the country at the time? Did this lead to extra trouble when he was out on the town? 'Well, I don't walk into pubs and walk up to people if I think they want a fight,' said Best. 'A lot of people think I do. I used to. I've always had that, if I walk into a bar or a club; it happens all the time. You know, there's always someone wants to come up and hit you over the head with a pint and go to work on Monday morning and tell their mates about it. And I used to put up with this, but if they're going to walk up and threaten you with a pint, if you smack them in the mouth first, they're not going to go to work and tell their mates that – you've got a black eye and a bloody nose, why? I've been hit over the head by a 55-year-old woman. In a club! She walked up and hit me over the head with her handbag. With a 55-year-old woman, though, what can you say, what can you do? You've just got to sit there and take it.'

Michael would have related to this feeling. He has often

said that he tends to avoid pubs after the fall of darkness due to the madness that sometimes sets in among the drinking crowd. Here again was the dovetailing of his pre-eminence in his field with that of his guest. As he was at the top of his profession, the King of Chat indeed, he could relate to the pressures and joys others face. However, to complete the circle of perfection, Michael has always retained the common touch. This combination of an awareness of the realities of fame and fortune with the down-to-earth Yorkshire nature made him the ultimate go-between for the chat show.

Not to mention the ultimate interviewer for Best, in particular. In 1975, Michael published a book about his pal, *George Best: An Intimate Biography*. Affectionate, yet honest, it was lapped up by admirers. During one appearance Best went on to talk more about the trappings of fame and the jealous reactions sometimes produced in people. 'I built my own image up first of all. And then I was sorry for it. I mean, just to go out anywhere at night and just sit and watch a show and just have an enjoyable evening, and 99 per cent of the time you know that when you come out, someone will have slashed your tyres or run into the car with 6-in nails. It's hard to take.'

By the time of his appearance on the show in the 1990s, footballers were earning far, far more money than even the superstar during the peak of his remarkable career. Not that he was resentful. He told Michael: 'People ask me if I regret that I didn't make the same sort of money as today's players. Listen, good luck to them! It's a short life and you never know from one day to the next. I still pay and watch them play. I think the Premiership's been absolutely wonderful.'

There were also plenty of laughs during the interviews. Best always had a knack for a funny story or turn of phrase, and Michael was great at teasing them out of him. He once asked him: 'What was the nearest to kick-off that you made love to a woman?' He replied: 'Er, I think it was half-time, actually.' This brought the house down and became much quoted for the rest of his life. Again, Michael had been the man to bring the tale out. Best then added the story of when he was caught by manager Wilf McGuinness in a clinch with a woman. 'He actually caught me in a lady's room just before we left for a Cup semi-final. The problem was that as he was leaving, he said: "You'd better play well today," and the first time I got the ball I fell flat on my face.' Again the audience absolutely loved every moment of those saucy soccer stories.

Best's battle with the booze was never a topic that Michael shirked from raising, nor one that he himself resented discussing with his favourite interviewer. 'The drinking wasn't a problem at first,' he told Michael. 'When you're 19 or 20 you can get pissed on a few drinks and it doesn't seem to matter. That's how it started with me. I had one golden rule: I never went out on a Friday night. I used to drink vodka and lemonade because it looked like nothing, and if any nosy sod rang the boss up and told him they'd seen me drinking in a club, I could always say it was lemonade. In the end those kind of pressures used to get me down. Whereas once I'd get silly drunk, I'd just get nasty drunk because I knew that someone would try something silly. I used to go for training pissed as a fart. Ten in the morning and I'd be drunk. Paddy Crerand used to say to me, "You smell like a brewery," and have a right go at me. But it didn't make any difference.'

It was a vivid recollection of his descent into dark times. However, the greatest story Michael ever elicited from Best is an amusing, upbeat one that has since gone down in history. Again, here is Parkinson at the forefront of the legend that has grown around someone he interviewed. The story concerns a trip that Best made to Las Vegas. To say the very least, it turned into quite an evening. Over to you, Bestie...

'By the end of the evening I was up $15,000 (it may have been $30,000) and Mary was getting a little tired. I decided to cash in my chips and go up to the room. I got a cab to our hotel with $15,0000/$30,000 in cash on me and as I went past the desk clerk, I ordered a magnum of champagne from the night porter. "Jesus, it's yourself," the night porter said to me. "I'll be right up, Mr Best, with your champagne."

'We took the elevator and Mary went for a shower to get ready for bed. I took out all the cash and spread it all over the bed. A few minutes later the little Irish guy taps on the door and I let him in. His eyes nearly popped out of his head when he saw all that money on the bed. As he put the champagne on the table, Miss World came into the room in a lovely see-thru baby-doll nightdress and the little Irish guy's eyes were now on stalks. I poured him out a glass of champagne, as well as one for Mary Stavin and me.

'We toasted each other and when he had finished his

glass, I put $200 on his tray and he said goodnight and thanks. As he was about to leave the room, he looked back at Miss World in her negligée and then at all the money on the bed, and then back at me and shook his head slowly from side to side. Before he slipped out the door, he put down his empty glass and he gave me one more sort of pitying look and said, "Where did it all go wrong, Georgie? Where did it all go wrong?"'

This story has become as associated with George Best, as has the beautiful, flowing silky football he played for clubs including Manchester United, Stockport County, Fulham, Hibernian and Northern Ireland. Best's and Michael's careers coincided and complemented one another. When he died in 2005, Parkinson was one of the first to pay tribute. 'The only tragedy George Best had to confront,' he concluded, 'is that he will never know how good he could have been.' Later, he added a more fulsome obituary. Writing in the *Daily Telegraph*, he offered: 'Matt Busby loved talking about George Best. He never worked him out, but he loved him. One day, just before Matt died, he said to me: "I keep having this terrible thought that one day George will end it all, that he'll commit suicide." He was right. It just took him longer than either of us thought.

'George knew what was happening. Ten years ago he confided: "A doctor friend once told me that one day I'd wake up and either switch on life or switch it off." And that is what he did. Why? The easy explanation is he was a chronic alcoholic. That's what killed him, but why did he drink so much? In all the time I knew him and all the hours we talked, he never said. He would sidestep the question with a joke. But drinking didn't make him happy. So why? I used to think it was because he was bored. He was the supremely gifted athlete who found playing football a simple matter. So was finding a mate. Women offered themselves and he took them, simple as that. No sweat. He had a sharp intelligence, but strangely little confidence in displaying it in the early years. In his maturity, even when the booze had taken hold, it was possible to glimpse what might have been.'

He then recalled the final time the pair met. It was a couple of months before Best's death in 2005. He had persuaded him to attend a reunion of players who had appeared alongside him for Manchester United. 'He sat all evening without a drink and reminisced. He said to me later it was one of the most enjoyable occasions he could remember,' says Michael. 'I said, "That's because you were sober." He said, "Whatever, I was certainly very happy." And I thought, not for the first time, maybe, just maybe, we'd got him back. A week later he was drinking again and the final spiral of his life had begun. When I sat down to write his obituary it occurred to me that I had been doing so for the past 15 years or so, in the sense that everything I wrote about him in that time seemed like a valediction.'

The death of George Best was a huge loss. Through his darkest days, Michael endeavoured to support the football legend. Despite the tragic end to his life, Best remains one of the key guests to appear on *Parkinson* down the years. It is also worth noting that despite his ability to appear on television when drunk – an interview with Terry Wogan on *Wogan* being a particularly memorable example – he never paid Michael the disrespect of coming onto *his* show drunk. It was a tribute, of sorts, to the respect in which he held him.

James Cagney

'I never imagined when I was a child watching the movies that I would ever meet James Cagney, but I did,' Michael once said. The Academy-award winning actor James Cagney was a guest that he has singled out as one of his all-time favourites. 'When I interviewed James Cagney, it was the first time he'd ever been interviewed,' says Michael. It is testimony to his abilities that anyone watching his interviews with the Hollywood legend would not have known this was the case. From that very first meeting, Michael's interviews with him became gripping, epochal encounters. Born in July 1899, Cagney is one of the movie world's most iconic actors. In 1999 the American Film Institute ranked him eighth among the Greatest Male Stars of All Time. Having spent much of the 1920s as a song-and-dance man in Vaudeville and onstage in New York, he then starred as a gangster in the 1931 film, *The Public Enemy*.

By the time he appeared on *Parkinson* in the 1970s, Cagney was an absolute legend. However, television interviews were for him a new territory. This was part of a seismic cultural shift of which Michael was at the forefront. 'When I started doing the talk show, there were huge stars that you never saw on television and had never been on television: James Cagney was one, Fred Astaire was another,

Robert Mitchum, James Stewart, John Wayne... They didn't do television.' Therefore, he was bursting with pride and joy at the fact that he was the first man to be able to interview these characters, particularly Cagney. 'There was a kind of excitement generated because they were these mythical figures who would appear at the top of the stairs: "Ladies and gentlemen, James Cagney."' He was to announce just that when cinema's quintessential tough guy appeared on his show in the 1970s, alongside fellow actor and friend Pat O'Brien.

Michael asked the pair: 'How did you meet?' O'Brien replied, 'In 1926, in New Jersey. I was playing in a stock company, a lowly young actor trying to get a break along the way. I was on a donut hunt for a long time. And there was a play that came along, the name of this play was, *Women Go On Forever*. And I'd been told there was a young fellow in it who looked like a future star. I'd read things about him. I just made up my mind I wanted to meet him.' O'Brien continued, becoming notably emotional along the way. 'I went backstage. Jim and I... Jim's an introvert, I'm an extrovert – I'm an Irish show-off, I like to be on all the time. So I took a shot in the dark, hoping I would meet this fellow. And he was just as kindly then... [chokes back tears] and as wonderful as he is today. That was 1926 and it's a friendship that's endured for 55 years.'

Michael then took the interview in another direction, adding a cheeky moment of banter while he was at it. 'You talked there about being different. One of the stories I've heard is that you used to go out all night and stay out in the town, and he used to go to be early. Is that true?' He then added, to considerable laughter, 'Does it still happen?' O'Brien replied: 'Oh, no! 31 and 81, there's a lot of difference, believe me.' Michael then turned to the fact that both actors were big news during America's gangster era. With an excited, almost boyish, smile, he asked: 'Did you ever meet any real gangsters?' This prompted another of Parkinson's most memorable early-day anecdotes. 'A funny thing happened. I was up at a horse show in Connecticut, and a little red-haired kid, freckled all over his face,' said Cagney. 'He came up and stood beside me. I didn't know him – I'd never seen him before. I said, "Hello, son." He said, "Well, did you or didn't you?" And I said, "Did I or didn't *what*? I don't know what you're talking about." He said, "Did you go yellow when you went to the chair that time?"'

Michael asked Cagney about the most famous line attributed to him: 'Did you ever say, "You dirty rat?"' To the surprise of many, Cagney replied: 'Never. No, I kind of assume that I must have suggested it somewhere along the line. But I do think that the dead end picked it up.' He then moved on to another of Cagney's trademarks, the hunched shoulder-flick mannerism that was so associated with him. 'You're the most imitated man in the world, I would imagine. What about the mannerisms, the sort of shoulder?' Cagney revealed where the shoulder flick came from. 'Well, all those things... see in vaudeville, you try to give the people something to get hold of,' he said. 'And this thing that I did was something I saw a fellow on 78th Street and First Avenue do, oh ages ago. And that's all he did! He didn't have a... he never worked for a living.' Michael joined in the general laughter and said: 'But he made a living out of doing that?!'

Cagney returned to *Parkinson* for another memorable interview in the 1980s. He began by talking about his childhood and turned to the topic of social class. 'It was a middle-class neighbourhood where I was born – middle-class, and every now and then they spotted a family who had produced a tough one. I wasn't a tough one – I had a mother who stopped all that nonsense. I was fairly handy with my fists; that's not hard. Everybody was a streetfighter. In order to get along you had to fight your way through. I recall one fight: three fights, one after the other. Third one, the boy and I went in again, and the result was interesting because I hit him on the bridge of the nose with my right hand and broke my hand. He was as tough as tough. He was just a very nice guy, but he was tough as could be. The guys were tough there and they learned how to take care of themselves. The girls could do it, too. My girl, Maud, was a left-handed girl, and she could punch her way through a brick wall. She was really something to cope with.'

It was a remarkable career by any standards. However, the way Cagney started surprised many people when Michael teased it out of him on *Parkinson*. 'My first job was in vaudeville. It was – are you ready? As a female impersonator. That was an act that had five fellows and five girls, and I jumped into the act on a Monday and I was with them for about three months. It was just another way of making $35 a week. Vaudeville taught me everything. You see, anything that came along, you grabbed it. It didn't matter what it was – a straight act, a sketch of a musical act – whatever, you did it all. Dancing was something you got right from the sidewalks. Everybody would dance. I don't know if I was just naturally gifted, but if it's there to do, I try to do it. Tap dancing? That's easy. It was nothing really – a lot of hard I work, I may say, but it was still easy. I wanted to make a movie with Fred Astaire. Years ago, Freddie and I had a kind of common agreement where he said, "Let's do one," and I said, "Fine," so we got it all set and nothing ever happened.'

So, why had he gone to vaudeville? Michael wondered aloud. 'I went there to get a job that paid living-room money – that was it, the sole idea involved. It wasn't so terribly different. Being in vaudeville, you were used to anything. Whatever came along, you grabbed it and did it; that was all. I used to write poetry, just little things that don't amount to anything. As the idea came along I'd just put it down in writing. You see, Bogart had a nervous habit of picking his nose – and he was a very nervous guy. I was driving north on Ventura Boulevard and he was driving south. So this thing, I didn't write it, I just said it: "In this silly town of ours, one sees odd preens and poses, but movie stars in fancy cars shouldn't pick their famous noses."'

Having played so many different roles, Cagney – by now warming to his theme and really relaxing into the conversation, as did so many of Michael's guests, thanks to his great ability as a host – closed in on the parts he most enjoyed. 'I find the tough guy in movies easy to play – it's a matter of turning back the clock, that's all, to my early days,' he said. 'The scripts for those films were just working scripts, the people who wrote them were workaday writers and they just made them up as they went along, and we improvised. I invented a lot of phrases – I didn't expect the writers to know those at all. There was a difference between Bogie and me. He came from a very nice family – they were entirely different from my family. He just used his head as a tough guy, he had to work at it.'

Fred Astaire

The last time Fred Astaire visited the UK, Michael Parkinson interviewed him. Before the cameras rolled, the host met his guest and noticed how nervous he was. To help him relax, Parkinson related the story of how when he was young, he tried to imitate the Astaire walk. Unable to do this, he then opted for the gait of John Wayne. As the band struck up, Michael descended the steps to his chair, tripping and ending up in an undignified heap at the bottom. Having reassured Astaire, Michael probably made him even more comfortable with this hilarious slip-up. Afterwards, Astaire quipped, 'Guess you got me mixed up with The Duke!'

Whether it was the pep talk or the stair-slip, Michael managed to relax Astaire into a great mood. He gave a revealing interview to *Parkinson* viewers in which he described how his career started and developed. It made for interesting viewing and remains one of Michael's favourite-ever interviews. 'I started at the age of 4?, and if you add it up, I have been performing professionally for 71 years. I wasn't forced into it – I went with my sister Adele to New York. I don't think anyone thought I was going to do anything: I just went because my sister was going to dance at school – stage school – and I went along too, and the first thing you know I was in it.'

He continued: 'I was glad my sister did retire because she didn't want to work any more. It wasn't easy to get her to rehearse. I'd say we ought to try that step over again and she'd say why? So she'd come out, I'd warm up a little bit and she'd do a few little nothing exercises and she wanted to retire, and it was fine. Then when I did get on [TV] and [become] something myself, everybody missed her very much because she was a very, very successful girl, a very good comedienne – she was wonderful. We got along great. She's marvellous today, I see her all the time.'

It was not until fairly late in life that he turned his dancing feet towards the world of cinema, as he told Michael: 'I was 34 when I went into the movies. It was an area that was unexplored in terms of dance at that time. There were a lot of things that we brought into it – fortunately people said it made it better. Whatever that was, it was nice to know. I always know that I loved the movies – I loved working in them and I still do. Sometimes you get an idea from the choreographer (I had a number of different ones) but I had quite a few myself, naturally. I could never sleep past four o'clock in the morning for some reason, and I'd lie there and think up something. I remember that one of the particular things I got at that hour was the *Top Hat* number. My sister had the room next to mine and I was up, and there was an umbrella standing in the corner of my room and I was making a noise, and my mother said, "What the hell are you doing in there?" So I said, "Oh sorry, I got an idea." She says, "Well, sleep on it, will you?" My mother said I should retire when I was 34. She said, "Well, you started so early and it's about time." She was such a wonderful woman, she had these cute ideas, and I said, "I'm afraid it isn't going to be possible" and that was all there was of that.'

In 1989, when Michael was asked who he would like to interview next, his reply showed just how much of a favourite Astaire had been. 'I don't want to sound arrogant, but my problem is who is there left to do?' he said. 'If the producer came to me and said we're going to get Kylie Minogue and Jason Donovan on because they're the biggest stars in the world, frankly I would not feel the same way about interviewing them as I did about Fred Astaire.' Thank goodness he refused to listen to his mother and quit at 34! Also, that Michael refused to succumb to his father's pressure to join Yorkshire Cricket Club. Though cricket-mad Michael might have been proud to represent Yorkshire, he has instead enjoyed a remarkable career in journalism and television, culminating in decades of hosting *Parkinson*, from which the above five golden guests are drawn. However, in truth any number of the 2,000 people that he has quizzed on the show could have made a claim to be in that same category.

He might be heading towards the winter of his life, but Michael remains a fan of summer. 'I was put on earth to stand in shafts of sunlight,' he says. 'That I have lived all my life in a mostly grey, damp and chilly land only goes to prove that you can't win 'em all.' Into retirement, he remains content and happy: 'In the end I shall be happy because I'll be giving myself something I've not had since I was 16 when I started work – the freedom to do whatever I want.'

His army of admirers will wish him well with his newfound freedom. A television legend and a natural treasure, he is a remarkable man. Arise, Sir Michael Parkinson.

APPENDICES

Television Filmography

Here are the main TV credits for Michael Parkinson's career as a presenter:

Cinema	1964
Parkinson	1971–2007
The Woofits	1980
TV-am/Good Morning Britain	1983
Give Us A Clue	1983–89
All Star Secrets	1984
Parkinson: One To One	1987–88
Help Squad	1991
Ghostwatch	1992
Going for a Song	1995
Auntie's All Time Greats	1996

Awards

1972   *Sun* Performer of the Year
1975   Best-Dressed Man On Radio
1998   Variety Club Personality of the Year
        Yorkshireman of the Year
        Music Industry Trust Services To Music
        Sony Radio Award
        Press Gazette Sports Writer of the Year
1999   Honorary doctorate from the University of
        Lincolnshire and Humberside
        Cover Magazine Best Sports Writer
        Parliamentary Beer Club Beer Drinker of the Year
        Fellow of the British Film Institute
2000   Companion of the British Empire (CBE) for
        services to broadcasting
2006   Honorary Patronage of the University
        Philosophical Society (Trinity College, Dublin)
2008   Knight Bachelor